Ways of Warriors, Codes of Kings

Lessons in Leadership from the Chinese Classics

TRANSLATED BY

Thomas Cleary

Shambhala
Boston & London
2000

SHAMBHALA PUBLICATIONS, INC.
Horticultural Hall
300 Massachusetts Avenue
Boston, MA 02115
www.shambhala.com

9 8 7 6 5 4 3 2

Printed in the United States of America

∞ This edition is printed on acid-free paper that meets the
American National Standards Institute Z39.48 Standard.
Distributed in the United States by Random House, Inc.,
and in Canada by Random House of Canada Ltd

The Library of Congress catalogues the hardcover edition of this book
as follows:
Ways of warriors, codes of kings: lessons in leadership from the
Chinese classics/translated by Thomas Cleary.
p.   cm.
ISBN 1–57062–443–7
ISBN 1–57062–569–7 (pbk.)
1. Military art and science—China—Early work to 1800.
2. Strategy. 3. Leadership. I. Cleary, Thomas F., 1949–   .
U101.W3   1999   98-39906
355.2—dc21   CIP

WAYS OF WARRIORS
CODES OF KINGS

Contents

Introduction · xi

Harmony First · 1
Four Corners · 1
Government · 2
Winning and Losing · 2
Occasions for Warfare · 3
Good Management · 3
When to Avoid Conflict · 4
When Attack is Feasible · 4
Victory Is Made by Order · 5
Life and Death · 6
Education and Training · 6
Generalship · 6
Assessing Opponents · 7
Management, Not Magic · 8
Order · 9
Organization · 9
Recruiting Talent · 10

The Consciousness
    of Society · 10
Fundamentals · 11
Influence Without
    Aggression · 12
Basic Tasks · 12
Inscrutability · 13
When to Act · 13
Leadership · 13
Preparation · 13
Prudence · 14
Diplomatic Debilitation · 14
The Hidden Key · 14
Winning Wars · 14
Spirit · 15
Orders · 15
Trust · 16
Inspiration by
    Example · 16

Group Integrity · 17

The Heart · 17

Affection and Respect · 18

Overflowing and Leaking · 18

Respect and Disrespect,
Victory and Defeat · 18

Trust and Efficiency · 19

Psychological Weaknesses · 19

Fighting · 20

Winning · 20

Defense · 20

Definitions · 21

Ethics of Warfare · 21

Priorities · 22

Business · 22

Punishment and Reward · 23

The Burden of Leadership · 23

Incompetence · 24

Perils of Power · 24

Cohesion and Consistency · 24

Manners of Warriors · 25

Command · 25

Order · 26

Subjectivity and Egoism · 26

Getting Information · 26

Bribery · 27

Social and Political Order · 27

The Prison Population · 27

Rulership and
Administration · 28

Economic
Fundamentalism · 29

Lapse · 29

Emperors · 30

Kings of Yore · 30

Total Dedication · 30

Qualities of Governments · 30

Strategy and Force · 31

Aggressiveness · 31

Supremacy without
Combat · 32

Severe Penalties · 32

Mutual Surety System · 33

Extreme Teamwork · 34

Wartime Discipline · 35

Timeliness · 35

Three Handicaps in War · 36

Sending People to War · 36

Twelve Ways of Winning
Victory · 36

The Art of the Attack · 38

Targeting Priorities · 38

Causing the People
to Thrive · 38

Morality of Warfare · 39

Martial and Cultural
Functions · 39

Conscript Armies · 39

Unity · 40

Calmness · 40

Desertion · 40

Enforcing Performance · 40

Three Excellences · 41

Motivation · 41

Common Cause · 42

Soft and Hard · 42

The Subtle · 42

Adaptation · 43

CONTENTS

Coordination · 43

Case by Case · 43

Military Methods · 44

Respect and Remuneration · 45

Following Orders · 45

Going Stale · 45

Organization and
Authority · 46

Effects of Attitude · 46

The Character of a
Commander · 47

Advice and Planning · 47

Confidentiality, Unity, and
Alacrity · 48

Leaks, Gaps, and Bribes · 48

Flaws in Commanders · 48

Psychological and Material
Inducements · 49

Knowing the Enemy · 49

Benefits and Popularity · 49

Oppression · 50

Corruption · 50

Powerful Clans · 50

Damage and Harm · 51

Subtle Strategy · 51

The Evolution of
Government · 52

Integrity and Dignity · 53

Fascism · 53

Conscience · 53

Subterfuge and Secrecy · 53

The Strategy of Hegemons · 54

Three Levels of Strategy · 54

Benevolence · 55

Mastery of Body and Mind · 56

Teaching Others · 56

Planning, Relaxation, and
Security · 57

Values · 57

Directives, Orders, and
Policies · 58

Near and Far · 58

Good and Bad · 59

Uncertainty and Confusion · 59

Equality by Purity · 59

Pure People · 60

Sagacious Gentlemen · 60

Insiders and Outsiders · 60

Pretenders and Proxies · 61

Promoting the Wise · 61

Cohesion · 61

The Way of Ancient Sages · 62

Wealth and Welfare · 62

Benevolence and Duty · 63

Demand and Supply · 63

Leadership and Quality of
Life · 63

Demeanor · 64

Arbitrary Approval · 64

Bases of Democracy · 64

Six Elements of Defense · 64

How to Preserve Territory · 65

Six Parasites · 65

Seven Harmful Things · 66

Duties · 67

The Way of the Dragon · 67

Anger · 68

False Reputation · 68

Appointing the Worthy · 69

Awards and Punishments · 69

The Way of Warfare · 69

Swift Response · 70

Reciprocity · 70

Subtleties of Strategy · 71

Symptoms of Sickness · 71

Efficiency · 71

People · 72

Nonviolent Attack · 72

Governing the World · 74

Fair Trade · 74

Playing Hardball · 75

Domesticating People · 76

Capacities of Commanders · 76

Excesses in Commanders · 76

Warfare · 78

Appearance and Reality · 78

Penalties and Prizes · 80

Top Talent · 81

Certainty and Secrecy · 81

Halving the Work · 81

Advantage and Timing · 82

Foresight · 82

Signs of Strength and
Weakness · 82

Humanity and Justice · 83

Love and Awe · 83

Caring for Both Sides · 84

Militarism and Defense · 84

Preparedness · 84

Ethics of Ancient Warriors · 84

Government by Enlightened
Virtue · 85

The Government of Wise
Kings · 85

Commands to the Troops of an
Invading Army · 86

Central and Local Authority
(1) · 87

Central and Local Authority
(2) · 87

Duties · 88

Education and Training · 88

Civil and Military
Organization · 88

Unaffected People · 89

Employment · 89

Security and Victory · 89

Sternness and Strictness · 90

Relaxation · 90

Statecraft and Military
Affairs · 91

Virtues and Skills · 91

Deterioration of Charisma · 92

Immediate Feedback · 92

Humility · 92

Failure and Fault · 93

Harmony · 93

Preparations · 94

Five Considerations · 94

Strategic Measurements · 95

Subterfuge · 96

Contingency Planning · 96

Efficiency · 97

Balance · 97

Economic Consequences of
Warfare · 98

Keeping Intact · 98

Foiling Opponents · 98

Four Levels of Attack · 99

Planning Attack · 99

Firmness and
Stubbornness · 99

Knowing Winners · 99

Invincibility and
Vulnerability · 100

Inconspicuous Success · 101

Victory and Defeat · 101

Organization and
Operation · 102

Surprise Tactics · 102

Momentum · 102

Paradox and Logic · 103

Maneuvering Others · 103

Disposition of Force · 103

Taking a Stand · 104

Seducing Enemies · 104

Successful Attack and
Defense · 105

Advance and Retreat · 105

Concentration and
Division · 105

Disabling Defenses · 106

Examining Enemies · 106

Form · 107

Formlessness · 107

Intelligence Needs · 108

Spirit and Heart · 108

Strength and Adaptation · 108

Rules for Military
Operations · 109

Introduction

For more than two thousand years, ever since Greece and Rome began importing silk from China, there has been a stream of transmission in arts and sciences East to West. Sometimes sinking underground in deserts of political isolation and warfare, sometimes springing to life in oases of new hybrid civilizations, over the centuries this stream of knowledge produced many technical innovations in material culture—in medicine, metallurgy, ceramics, papermaking, textiles, agriculture, pyrotechnics, printing, transport, mathematics, astronomy.

Many seminal forms of social and political science are also found in the works of the ancients—theocracy, bureaucracy, hierarchy, monarchy, plutarchy, oligarchy, feudalism, imperialism, militarism, despotism, fascism, legalism, anarchism, socialism, paternalism, individualism, conformism—these conceptions and more were all articulated by Chinese political philosophers of olden times. Even revolutionary and democratic ideas are to be found in Chinese lore of more than two thousand years ago, as are more subtle spiritual conceptions of state, society, and individuality.

Ideas tend to travel with trade, as with diplomacy and warfare, often taking on new forms as they are transformed by new environments and applied to new situations, expressed in different languages, and adapted by diverse peoples. It is not always possible to track cultural drift, especially in the shifting sands of global events, but it is clear that for all the variety of world civilizations, we share intersecting histories and have common interests.

Among the spheres of Chinese culture that have attracted the attention of other peoples near and far, past and present, the sciences of statecraft and warfare have been particularly prominent. Many of the Asian nations, incuding Korea, Japan, Tibet, Vietnam, and various Mongolian, Turkic, and Tungusic nations of north and central Asia, rose to peaks of political power employing Chinese methods of organization and operation.

These techniques were probably brought west from China long ago by the Huns, who were longtime major trading partners, territorial rivals, and both enemies and allies of the Chinese. The eastern Huns eventually joined the Chinese empire, and the western Huns headed west, where, centuries later, under the infamous Attila, they briefly terrorized Europe before settling down.

Marco Polo undoubtedly also brought some knowledge of these matters back to Italy after his travels in China in the fourteenth century. The resemblances of many of the ideas of sixteenth-century Machiavelli to Chinese political and military strategists' may derive from information gathered by Marco Polo, or later by Jesuit missionaries. This knowledge was also obtained by the princes of Muscovy, who laid the foundations of the Russian empire in the fourteenth and fifteenth centuries. The Russians learned these principles from their erstwhile Mongol-Tatar masters, the Golden Horde. This was the western branch of the great Mongolian empire, which had taken over the rulership of China in the thirteenth century.

In the latter eighteenth century, a French Jesuit scholar made an early literary attempt to introduce Chinese strategic lore in Western Europe. Interest in Eastern mysticism was peaking in France at that time, and the French cleric's treatment of Chinese tactical literature emphasized the humanistic elements of the material. Deriving from the Taoist background, this aspect of classical Chinese strategic lore was an intriguing surprise to Western observers.

During the nineteenth century, Europe and America were more concerned with exploiting China materially than studying Chinese civilization, yet there were secular thinkers of the West who developed a sympathetic and even admiring interest in the Confucian idea of a state governed by learned philosophers and poets. This aspect of Chinese culture seemed consonant with familiar classical ideals of Greek philosophers and was also close to the Celtic tradition once dominant in Europe and ardently admired by many scholars of the late nineteenth century. Not seeming to require specific religious belief, Confucianism presented Western secularists with an interesting contrast to the religious sectarianism infesting European politics.

The emergence of modern Japan as an international military and economic power, heralded by the defeat of imperial China and Russia at war in 1895 and 1905, renewed Western interest in traditional Chinese strategic literature. Japan was one of the principal heirs of Chinese culture, and its meteoric rise to power in modern times strengthened Western interest in the effects of certain social values and organizational techniques transmitted through the heritage of Chinese philosophies, including the peculiar combination of Confucian idealism and tactical pragmatism.

Widespread Western interest in Chinese culture today is due in part to recent historical events and contemporary political and demographic conditions, but it is also a natural continuation of a complex trend of centuries' standing. The East-West polarization of the last five hundred years has not inhibited either trade or cultural exchange, even if it has created acrimony and violence.

It is the spells of interruption and ignorance, however prolonged, that ought to be regarded as anomalous, rather than contact and interchange. Acrimony and violence may be more dramatic and exciting than humane interest and understanding, but the passage of time has shown that when the dust clears in the aftermath of conflict on the stage of history, no matter who wins or loses, former enemies always learn to learn more about each other.

The rise of modern China on the international scene has stimulated increased interest in Chinese civilization, particularly in the strategic and tactical lore so prized in the fields of statecraft, diplomacy, military affairs, and commerce. The problems of balancing partnership and rivalry in an inherently competitive international theater are among the foremost concerns of world leaders in business and politics as we enter the twenty-first century.

While misunderstandings may naturally arise concerning different ways of seeing and doing things, nevertheless, as nations and peoples continue to take constructive interest in one anothers' cultures and philosophies of life, the foundation for mutual understanding and conflict resolution will continue to develop. With the growth of the world population, the power of modern technology, and the proliferation of deadly weaponry, these conceptual facilities for mediation and cooperation become ever more critical to the survival and prosperity of human society.

This book contains an anthology of selections translated from several famous works of classical Chinese strategic lore. Some of the ideas are easily applied to current conditions, some of them are more like warnings. All are about human potential, for better and for worse. There are many organizational concepts in this lore that are equally applicable within different political and social contexts, while there are others that essentially illustrate drastic and dubious measures taken by tyrants.

Through observation of the whole range of human possibilities, for good and for bad, moral and practical acumen can be developed. Through cultivation of moral and practical acumen, powers of independent decision and choice can be attained. The excitable observer will pass judgment first and then make knowledge conform to judgment; the prudent observer will first learn to know and then judge according to knowledge.

Whether it is in the domain of statecraft, or military action, or commerce, or social, familial, and interpersonal relations, empathic understanding of human nature and behavior is crucial to successful and satisfying interaction. In classical literature designed to help us attain human understanding in all of its aspects, here and there we may see reflections of ourselves or others as we are and act. We may also see how effective we or others could become if we tried, or what ill could become of us all if we were too careless to avoid it. Thus we can find that there are important and useful things for us to learn along the whole spectrum of human possibilities, pieces of insight that can help us on our way.

WAYS OF WARRIORS
CODES OF KINGS

Harmony First

When there is disharmony in a nation, it cannot launch an army. When there is disharmony in an army, it cannot set forth a battlefront. When there is disharmony in a battlefront, it cannot proceed into combat. When there is disharmony in combat, victory cannot be assured.

Therefore when rulers who have the Way are going to mobilize their people, they first establish harmony before major undertakings.

Wu Qi's Art of War

Four Corners

The Way is for returning to fundamentals and going back to beginnings. Duty is for doing business and achieving success. Strategy is for avoiding harm and gaining advantages. Contracts are for protecting business and preserving achievements.

If their actions do not conform to the Way and their undertakings do not accord with duty, those in important positions of high rank will inevitably get into trouble.

Therefore sages guide people with the Way, manage them with duty, show them how to behave with decorum, and treat them with humaneness. If you cultivate these four virtues, you thrive, while if you neglect them you decline.

Wu Qi's Art of War

GOVERNMENT

Whether governing a nation or an army, it is imperative to teach people decorum, inspire them with duty, and cause them to have a sense of shame.

Wu Qi's Art of War

WINNING AND LOSING

When people have a sense of shame, in great countries that is sufficient for combat, in small countries it is sufficient for defense.

However, it is easier to win by fighting than it is to win by defense.

Therefore it is said that of the warring states in the land, those who win five victories will be a disaster, those who win four victories will be exhausted; those who win three victories will be hegemons, those who win two victories will be kings; the one who wins one victory will be emperor.

So those who win the world by numerous victories are rare; those who perish thereby are many.

Wu Qi's Art of War

OCCASIONS FOR WARFARE

There are five occasions for warfare. First is fighting for honor. Second is fighting for profit. Third is accumulated antipathy. Fourth is internal disorder. Fifth is on account of famine.

They also have five names. The first is called a war of duty. The second is called a war of strength. The third is called a war of hardness. The fourth is called a war of violence. The fifth is called a war of rebellion.

Stopping violence and remedying chaos is called duty. Relying on the masses to attack is called strength. Mobilizing an army on account of rage is called hardness. Seeking profit by eliminating disorder is called violence. Initiating action and mobilizing the masses when the country is chaotic and the people are exhausted is called rebellion.

There is a tactic for each of these five. Duty must be overcome by courtesy. Strength must be overcome by modesty. Hardness must be overcome by talking. Violence must be overcome by deception. Rebellion must be overcome by strategy.

Wu Qi's Art of War

GOOD MANAGEMENT

If the leader can put worthy people in higher positions while keeping unworthy people in subordinate positions, then the battlefront is stable.

If the people are secure in their fields and houses and familiar with the local officials, then defense is secure.

When the people all approve of their own leadership and disapprove of the neighboring country, then war is already won.

Wu Qi's Art of War

3

WHEN TO AVOID CONFLICT

Avoid conflict with opponents when

1. their land is vast and their population is large;
2. their rulers care for the ruled, resulting in general welfare;
3. their rewards are reliable and punishments judicious, always timely;
4. they are ranked according to achievement on the battle line, with responsibilities entrusted to the worthy and tasks to the able;
5. their armed forces are massive and their weaponry is advanced;
6. they have help from neighbors all around and assistance from large countries.

If you do not match up to an enemy in these respects, avoid them unhesitatingly.

Wu Qi's Art of War

WHEN ATTACK IS FEASIBLE

It is imperative to examine the enemy's emptiness and fullness and aim for their vulnerabilities.

When enemies have newly arrived from afar, while their columns are still unsettled, they can be attacked.

When they have just eaten and have not yet made preparations, they can be attacked.

When they are running, they can be attacked.

When they are tired out, they can be attacked.

When they have not yet gotten an advantageous location, they can be attacked.

When they miss opportunities and things are not going smoothly for them, they can be attacked.

When they are stretched out endlessly on a long journey, they can be attacked.

When they are crossing water and have reached halfway, they can be attacked.

When they are in defiles or narrow roads, they can be attacked.

When their signals are confused, they can be attacked.

When their battle lines keep shifting, they can be attacked.

When their commanders alienate the officers and soldiers, they can be attacked.

When their hearts are afraid, they can be attacked.

Wu Qi's Art of War

VICTORY IS MADE BY ORDER

If rules and orders are unclear, rewards and penalties are unsure, and the troops do not stop and go on signal, even if you have a million of them, what is the use?

Order means having decorum when at rest; having dignity when on the move; being unopposable in advance, unpursuable in retreat, orderly in forward and reverse movements; responding to signals left and right: even if cut off they form battle lines, even if scattered they form columns. Whether in safety or danger, the troops can be joined but not divided, can be deployed but not exhausted. Wherever you hurl them, none in the world can stand up to them.

Wu Qi's Art of War

LIFE AND DEATH

A battlefield is a place where corpses are made. If you are sure you'll die, then you'll survive; if you have your heart set on getting out alive, then you'll die.

Good commanders are as if they were sitting in a leaking boat or lying under a burning roof: when they can baffle the planning of the intelligent and present no target for the rage of the brave, then they can take on opponents.

Wu Qi's Art of War

EDUCATION AND TRAINING

People always die for their inability and suffer defeat for their lack of training. Therefore education and discipline are priorities of the arts of war.

Wu Qi's Art of War

GENERALSHIP

One who has mastered both culture and warfare can be the commander of an army; one who can be both hard and soft can direct the military. Usually when people talk about military leaders, they consider their bravery, but bravery is only one fraction of military leadership. The fact is that brave men will readily clash; if they readily clash without knowing whether it will be advantageous, they are not yet competent.

So there are five things military leaders treat carefully: (1) order, (2) preparedness, (3) resoluteness, (4) discipline, (5) simplicity.

1. Order means governing many as effectively as governing few.
2. Preparedness means being as if you'll see your enemies the moment you step out your door.
3. Resoluteness means not thinking of living when facing the enemy.
4. Discipline means being as if only beginning to fight even when you have won.
5. Simplicity means that rules and orders are minimal and not overcomplicated.

To accept a mission without refusing, not considering returning until the opponent is broken—these are the manners of commanders. Therefore on the day an army goes out, there is death with glory rather than life with disgrace.

Wu Qi's Art of War

Assessing Opponents

It is essential in any war to figure out the other side's commander first, examining his abilities, employing strategy according to conditions. Then you will succeed without laboring.

If the commander is stupid and trusting, he can be deceived and seduced.

If he is greedy and shameless, he can be bribed and bought.

If he is mercurial and lacks strategy, he can be tired out.

If the upper classes are rich and arrogant while the lower classes are poor and resentful, they can be alienated and divided.

If they are hesitant in their movements and their troops have nothing to rely on, they can be stampeded.

If the officers disrespect their commander and want to go home, then block the highways and leave narrow roads open, where they can be ambushed.

Wu Qi's Art of War

MANAGEMENT, NOT MAGIC

King Wei of Liang asked Master Wei Liao, "Is it true that the Yellow Emperor punished and rewarded in such a way as to win all the time?"

Master Wei Liao said, "Attacking with punishment and maintaining with reward is not a matter of astrology, divination, or geomancy. The Yellow Emperor only attended to human management.

"Why? Suppose there is a city that cannot be taken by siege from east or west and cannot be taken by siege from north or south—could no one take advantage of it at an opportune moment? The reason it cannot be taken, however, is that the walls are high, the moats are deep, it is fully armed, it has abundant supplies of goods and grains, and the great men are of one mind. If the walls were low, the moats were shallow, and the defense were weak, then it would be taken. Seen in this way, astrology, divination, and geomancy are not as good as human management.

"According to *Celestial Agencies,* 'A battle formation with its back to water is a ground that is cut off; a battle formation facing a hill is a lost army.' Yet when King Wu attacked Emperor Zhou of the Shang dynasty, he set out his battle formation with its back to the Ji River, facing the mountain slopes; striking Zhou's 100,000 troops with 22,500 men, he destroyed the Shang dynasty. Was Zhou not in accord with the principles of battle formation given in *Celestial Agencies?*

8

"When Zixin, lord general of Chu, was at war with the men of Qi, a comet appeared with its tail pointed toward Qi. The direction of a comet's tail is supposed to indicate victory, suggesting that Qi should not be attacked. Lord Zixin said, 'What does a comet know! When people fight with brooms, the one who uses the broom backward wins.' The next day he engaged the men of Qi in battle and routed them.

"The Yellow Emperor said, 'Before spirits and before ghosts, first consult your own intelligence.' This refers to natural faculties, and is just a matter of human management.

"*Military Configurations* says, 'Ban soothsayers, and do not let them divine the fortunes of warfare for officials.'"

Master Wei Liao

ORDER

In any army, order must be established first; then the soldiers will not be unruly. When the soldiers are not unruly, discipline is clear. When you have a hundred troops all fighting according to directions, they can bring down columns and disrupt battlefronts; when you have a thousand troops all fighting, they can overthrow armies and kill their guards. When ten thousand troops align their blades, no one in the world can fight them.

Master Wei Liao

ORGANIZATION

It is said, "Appoint the intelligent, employ the capable, and business will show a profit before long; make rules clear and directions precise, and business will be auspicious without divination; honor achievement and support hard work, and prosperity will be attained without prayer."

It is also said, "The timing of the heavens is not as good as the advantage of the earth; the advantage of the earth is not as good as harmony among people." What sages value is human management.

Master Wei Liao

RECRUITING TALENT

If people say they have a way to overcome opponents, don't accept them on word alone—be sure to test their ability to fight. Have them take over someone else's land and govern some other people; make sure to bring in those who prove to be talented. If you cannot bring in talented people yet want to take over the world, you'll be overthrowing your own forces and killing your own commanders. This way, even if you win at war your country will grow weaker and weaker, and the more land you win the poorer your country will be. This lies within corruption of the internal organization of the nation.

Master Wei Liao

THE CONSCIOUSNESS OF SOCIETY

Social order makes the people unselfish. If the people are unselfish, the whole land is one family and there is no plowing or spinning for private personal purposes; they share cold and hunger in common. Therefore a household with ten sons has no more to eat, while a household with but one son has no less to eat. How could there be brawling and drunkenness to ruin good folk?

When the people are inconsiderate of one another, then greed arises, and problems of contention occur. When a leader becomes unruly, then the people have their own private stores of goods and their own caches of money; once people violate prohibitions, they are arrested and punished. Where are the qualifications to lead people?

Good governments organize their systems so as to get the people to be unselfish. If the common people do not presume to be selfish, then none will do wrong. Return to fundamentals, focus on principles, set forth on a unified course; then greed will leave, contention will stop, prisons will be empty. The fields will be full and cereals abundant, giving security to the people and consideration to those afar; then there will be no difficulties with the world outside and no violence or chaos within. This is the epitome of order.

Master Wei Liao

FUNDAMENTALS

Assess the relative fertility or barrenness of the soil to establish towns and build cities. Have the cities fit the land, let the land fit the population, let the population fit the produce. When these three fit each other, it is possible to keep secure within, and possible to win at war outside.

Land is the means of supporting the population, walled cities are the means of defending the land, warfare is the means of defending cities. Therefore if you see to the tilling, the populace will not hunger; if you see to defense, the land won't be imperiled; if you see to warfare, cities won't be surrounded.

Master Wei Liao

INFLUENCE WITHOUT AGGRESSION

Making clear what is forbidden and what is allowed, what will work and what will not, attract disenfranchised people and utilize unused land. If the land is extensive and put to use, the country grows rich; if the people are numerous and orderly, then the nation will be peaceful. A wealthy and peaceful nation can influence the global order without aggression.

Master Wei Liao

BASIC TASKS

We coordinate our directives and clarify our penalties and rewards, so that no one gets to eat without producing and no one attains rank without fighting, causing the people to compete enthusiastically in agriculture and warfare, so none in the world can oppose us.

These things were the basic tasks of ancient kings; among these basic tasks, warfare is most urgent. Therefore ancient kings focused on the military in five regards: if supplies are not abundant, then operations cannot be carried out; if rewards are not generous, then the people will not be encouraged; if warriors are not specially selected, the troops will not be strong; if equipment is not on hand, power will not be full; if penalties and rewards are not appropriate, the troops will not be wary. Those who see to these five things can maintain their holdings while at rest and can obtain what they want when they go into action.

When you are on the defense and go on the offense, your defense must be secure, your battle lines must be firm, your attacks must be all-out, and your combat must be coordinated.

Master Wei Liao

INSCRUTABILITY

When you master warfare, you are as though hidden in the earth, as if far out in space, emerging from nothing.

Master Wei Liao

WHEN TO ACT

A military operation should not be initiated in a state of excitement. If you see victory, then you mobilize; if not, you desist.

Master Wei Liao

LEADERSHIP

A commander is not ruled by heaven above, not ruled by earth below, and not ruled by other people. He is mellow and cannot be needled into anger; he is pure and cannot be bribed. If you let the crazy, blind, and deaf lead others, there's trouble!

Master Wei Liao

PREPARATION

When the trouble is within a hundred miles, you do not mobilize a day's force. If the trouble is within a thousand miles, you do not mobilize a month's force. When the trouble is global, you do not mobilize a year's force.

Master Wei Liao

PRUDENCE

If a bandit is swinging a sword in the middle of town, every-one will run away. I don't think that means one man is brave while everyone else is a bunch of cowards. Why? Because there's a difference between life and death.

Master Wei Liao

DIPLOMATIC DEBILITATION

The reason the nation is troubled is that valuable resources are spent on diplomatic presents, beloved children are sent out as diplomatic hostages, and territory is diplomatically ceded, in order to get reinforcements from all over. In name they may number a hundred thousand, but in reality they are not more than several tens of thousands. When those troops arrive, they all tell their commanders that there is no reason for them to be the first to fight. In reality, they are not able to fight.

Master Wei Liao

THE HIDDEN KEY

We put the world's goods to our own use, we organize the world's organizations for our organization.

Master Wei Liao

WINNING WARS

Wars might be won by strategy, by threat, or by force. When you cultivate military training and size up enemies so well as to cause them to lose their spirits so their armies dissolve, and though fully prepared you do not need to act, that is winning by strategy.

When you maintain precise order, make rewards and penalties clear, prepare equipment and supplies, and induce a fighting spirit in the people, that is winning by threat.

When you destroy armies and kill their commanders, storm ramparts and unleash catapults, expelling populations and taking their territories, returning only after succeeding, that is winning by force.

Master Wei Liao

Spirit

What enables commanders to go to war is the people; what enables the people to go to war is spirit. When they are full of spirit, they fight; when their spirit is taken away, they run.

There are five ways to dispirit enemies before setting upon them and clashing. First is the issue of strategy. Second is the issue of mobilization. Third is the issue of crossing borders. Fourth is the issue of fortification and defense. Fifth is the issue of formation and offense.

These five things should be put into action after first sizing up enemies so as to dispirit them by striking their gaps. Those who are skilled at warfare are able to dispirit others without being dispirited by others. Dispiriting is a mental mechanism.

Master Wei Liao

Orders

Orders are for unifying a multitude. If the multitude does not clearly understand, then there will be repeated changes; when there are repeated changes, even if orders are issued the multitude will not trust them.

Therefore the rule for giving orders is that they are not changed on account of minor errors and not reissued on account of minor questions. Thus when the leadership issues unhesitating orders, then the group listens with undivided attention; when it acts without hesitation, the group has no divided will.

Master Wei Liao

TRUST

Those who led the people in ancient times could never have gotten their power without winning their trust; they could never have gotten them to fight to the death without getting their power.

Therefore a nation must have principles of courtesy, faithfulness, and friendliness; then it can exchange hunger for sufficiency. A nation must have customs of respect, kindness, and modesty; then it can exchange death for life.

Those who led the people in ancient times put courtesy and faithfulness before rank and salary, modesty before discipline, and friendliness before regulation.

Master Wei Liao

INSPIRATION BY EXAMPLE

Those who make war must inspire their troops by their own example, like the mind employing the limbs. If they are not inspired, soldiers will not die for the cause; if the soldiers will not die for the cause, the army will not fight.

On a toilsome campaign, commanders must not put themselves first. In the heat they should not spread canopies, in the cold they should not double their clothing. On precipitous paths, they should dismount and walk; they should drink only after the troops' wells have been made, eat only after the soldiers' food has been cooked, and pitch camp only after the soldiers' camp is set. They must share the same hardship and ease; that way, even if the campaign goes on for a long time, the troops will not wane away or wear out.

Master Wei Liao

Group Integrity

A military force is firm when calm, victorious when united. Those whose power is divided are weak, those who are suspicious fall out: therefore they are not robust in their movements, and they let their enemies escape their grip.

The commanders, officers, and soldiers are like a body in their actions: when they have doubts and suspicions in their minds, then even if plans are determined, they are not acted on; and when action is decided on, there is no control. There are divergent opinions, empty talk, commanders without dignity and soldiers without discipline, guaranteed to fail if they launch a seige. This is called an unhealthy army, incompetent to fight.

Master Wei Liao

The Heart

The leader is the heart, the followers are the limbs and joints. If the heart acts truthfully, the limbs and joints will be strong; if the heart acts suspiciously, the limbs will rebel.

17

If the leadership is not disciplined of heart, the soldiery is not active of limb; even if they win a victory, it is a lucky win, not the strategy of the attack.

Master Wei Liao

AFFECTION AND RESPECT

You cannot employ people you cannot please; you cannot mobilize people you cannot impress by sternness. Where there is affection, underlings obey; where there is respect, leadership is established. Because of affection, there is no division; because of respect, there is no offense. Therefore leadership is a matter of affection and respect.

Master Wei Liao

OVERFLOWING AND LEAKING

A kingdom enriches its commoners, a hegemony enriches its gentry; a barely surviving nation enriches its grandees, a moribund nation enriches its treasury. That is called overflowing on top while leaking at the bottom—nothing will help when calamity comes.

Master Wei Liao

RESPECT AND DISRESPECT, VICTORY AND DEFEAT

When your people respect you, they disrespect your enemies; if they respect your enemies, they disrespect you. The one who is disrespected loses, while the one whose dignity is established wins. If the commanders are capable, the officers respect the commanders; when the officers respect the commanders, the common people respect the officers; when the common people respect the officers, their enemies respect those people. Therefore to know the course of victory and defeat, it is necessary to first know the workings of respect and disrespect.

Master Wei Liao

TRUST AND EFFICIENCY

If you are not sure of winning a battle, don't talk of fighting. If you are not sure to take the object of a siege, don't talk of attack. Otherwise, even if penalties and awards are announced, that cannot win trust.

Trust must be there before you can make plans; events must be foreseen before they happen. So a group that has gathered does not disperse without doing anything, an army that has gone forth does not come back without doing anything: they stalk enemies as one would look for a lost child, and strike enemies as one would save a drowning man.

Master Wei Liao

PSYCHOLOGICAL WEAKNESSES

Those imprisoned in narrow straits haven't the heart to fight; those who spoil for fights are deficient in spirit; those who are belligerent have no victorious army.

Master Wei Liao

FIGHTING

Whenever you fight for justice, the initiative should come from yourself.

You should engage in hostilities in private competition only when it cannot be helped.

When trouble arises from antagonism, you should not make the first move but wait and see what happens first. Therefore when there is a dispute, you should wait watchfully; while there is peace, you should prepare yourself.

Master Wei Liao

WINNING

Some military operations win victory at court, some win victory in the field, some win victory in the market. If you fight unsuccessfully but are lucky enough not to get beat, this is a partial victory by unexpectedly getting at an opponent's fears. Partial victory means it is not complete; one whose victory is incomplete is not known for strategy.

Master Wei Liao

DEFENSE

When on the defense, if you fight back without being able to advance beyond your own walls or retreat into your strongholds, that is not good. If you have all the warriors, armor, and weaponry concentrated inside your walls and then take in the storage depots and dismantle the houses of the people and bring them into the city, that will inflame the invaders' spirit while dampening the defenders' spirit. If the enemy attacks, it will cause a lot of casualties. Nevertheless, the commanders of the age do not know this.

Master Wei Liao

DEFINITIONS

Dignity is a matter of not changing. Generosity is a matter of timing. Cleverness is a matter of responding to events. Combat is a matter of mastering spirit. Attack is a matter of unexpectedness. Defense is a matter of external array. Impeccability is a matter of measure and calculation. Stamina is a matter of preparation. Prudence is a matter of wariness of the small. Wisdom is a matter of management of the great. Getting rid of pests is a matter of decisiveness. Winning followers is a matter of being humble to others.

Regret is in trusting the dubious. Evil is in massacre. Bias is in selfishness. Misfortune is in hating to hear one's own faults. Excess is in exhausting the wealth of the people. Unclarity is in admitting interlopers. Insubstantiality is in acting out too easily. Narrowmindedness is in alienating the intelligent. Calamity is in profiteering. Injury is in familiarity with petty people. Ruin is in not having any defense. Peril is in having no order.

Master Wei Liao

ETHICS OF WARFARE

In general, a military force is not to attack an inoffensive city and does not kill innocent people. To kill people's fathers and brothers, to profit from people's money and goods, and to enslave people's sons and daughters are all robbery.

Therefore the military is to execute the violent and unruly and to stop injustice. Where a military force attacks, the farmers do not leave their work in the fields, the merchants do not leave their shops, the officials do not leave their offices: since the target of the military is only the top man, the soldiers do not have to bloody their blades for everyone to be won over.

Master Wei Liao

PRIORITIES

A large country emphasizes farming and fighting; a middling country emphasizes relief and defense; a small country emphasizes business and livelihood. With farming and fighting, they don't seek external power; with relief and defense, they don't seek external help; with business and livelihood, they don't seek external resources.

Master Wei Liao

BUSINESS

Those who can neither fight nor defend should be assigned to business; business is a means of providing for warfare and defense. Even if a large country does not have reinforcements equivalent to a middling country, it will invariably have a market equivalent to a small country.

Master Wei Liao

PUNISHMENT AND REWARD

Penalties and rewards are means of showing martial prowess. If the armed forces can all be made to shudder at the execution of one man, kill him; if ten thousand people can be gladdened by awarding one man a prize, then give him a prize. The most impressive executions are of important people; the most impressive rewards are those given to lesser people.

When those who deserve to be executed are invariably executed even if they are high-ranking, important people, that means punishment reaches all the way upward; if awards are given even to cowherds and horse grooms, that means rewards flow downward. To be able to penalize the highest echelons and reward the lowest ranks is the martial prowess of a military commander; that is the reason leaders of men take commanders seriously.

Master Wei Liao

THE BURDEN OF LEADERSHIP

It is the military commanders who give the call to arms, deciding to fight when they face difficulty, engaging in combat with armies. If their call to arms is right, they are rewarded for their achievement and become famous; if their call is not right, then they themselves die and the country is ruined. The question of survival and ruin, security and peril, is the reason for the call to arms—how can military leadership not be considered a serious matter?

Master Wei Liao

INCOMPETENCE

An ancient said, "They attack without war chariots, defend without barbed wire." This refers to incompetent armies. When there is nothing to be seen or heard, it is because the country has no commercial organization. Commercial organization means management of goods. Buying cheap and selling dear constricts the people of the middle and lower classes. When the people look hungry and their horses are emaciated, what does this mean? The market has produce but its regulation is unsupervised. Any who run vast political systems without regulating commerce would not be considered able to do battle.

Master Wei Liao

PERILS OF POWER

A military commander is not controlled by heaven above, not controlled by earth below, not controlled by people in between. That is why armaments are instruments of ill omen, fighting is a vice, a general is an officer of death, and these are employed only when unavoidable. There is no heaven above, no earth below, no ruler behind, no adversary in front: an army that is as one man is like a wolf, like a tiger, like wind, like rain, like thunder, like lightning; when it rumbles ominously, the whole world is frightened.

Master Wei Liao

COHESION AND CONSISTENCY

Winning armies are like water. Water is extremely soft, but where it touches, even hills will be eroded by it, for no other reason than that it is cohesive by nature and its pressure is constantly applied.

Master Wei Liao

MANNERS OF WARRIORS

When Wu Qi warred with Qin, he didn't have bordered fields leveled for bunkers, he just used brushwood for cover against frost and dew. Why? Because he did not elevate himself over others. When you are asking people to die, you don't demand their reverence; when you are using people's strength, you don't complain of their manners.

Therefore in ancient times warriors in armor didn't bow, to show people that no one could put them to a lot of bother. I have never heard of a case, past or present, where anyone could bother people and hope to ask them to die and use all their strength!

Master Wei Liao

COMMAND

The day a general gets his orders, he forgets his home; when an army camps in the field, the troops forget their families; when the signal drum is sounded, they forget themselves.

When Wu Qi was overseeing a battle, an attendant presented a sword. Wu Qi said, "A general's only job is to give directions. Solving doubts in the face of trouble, conducting the troops and directing their blades—that is the work of a general. Wielding an individual sword is not the business of a general."

Master Wei Liao

ORDER

When Wu Qi was warring with Qin, before the armies clashed, one man who could not contain his boldness went out and took two enemy heads. When he came back, Wu Qi was going to execute him on the spot. The military inspector admonished him, "This is a talented soldier—he should not be executed." Wu Qi said, "He may be a talented soldier all right, but that was not my order." And he executed him.

Master Wei Liao

SUBJECTIVITY AND EGOISM

Military leadership is a directorate, in charge of myriads of people, so it is not to be affected by the subjective whims of one individual. If you are not an egomaniac, all sorts of people can come to you and you can organize them; all sorts of people can come to you and you can direct them.

Master Wei Liao

GETTING INFORMATION

If you carefully examine the circumstances, expressions, emotions, and states of mind of prisoners, then you can find out the truth about them without beating it out of them. If you flog people's backs, brand people's sides, and thumbscrew people's fingers, even among soldiers of national distinction there would be those who would make false confessions because they could not bear the torture.

Master Wei Liao

BRIBERY

There's a contemporary saying, "For a thousand pieces of gold, you won't be executed; for a hundred pieces of gold, you won't be imprisoned." Try to listen to my words and follow my methods: then even the smartest wits will not be able to speak a false word, and even if they had ten thousand pieces of gold they couldn't spend a bit in bribes.

Master Wei Liao

SOCIAL AND POLITICAL ORDER

Officials in charge of affairs are basic to social order. Organization means division of labor, which is part of social order. High ranks and large salaries must be fitting; that is the substance of hierarchy. Favoring the good, punishing the bad, and making census methods correct are tools for taking account of the populace. Equalizing land distribution and regulating taxes are standards of taking and giving. Regulating artisans and providing tools and equipment is the achievement of master craftsmen. Drawing boundaries and building barricades is for eliminating the suspicious and stopping the excessive and the obscene.

Master Wei Liao

THE PRISON POPULATION

Now those who are incarcerated number in the dozens in small jails, in the hundreds in middle-sized prisons, and in the thousands in large penitentiaries. Ten people are occupied in the custody of a hundred people, a hundred people are occupied in the custody of a thousand people, a thousand people are occupied in the custody of ten thousand people. Those who are in their custody are their relatives and brothers, their relatives by marriage, their acquaintances and friends.

So the farmers are taken away from their work in the fields, the merchants are taken away from their shops, the officials are taken away from their offices. Thus the law-abiding people involved are all in a state of incarceration. According to the laws of warfare, the mobilization of a force of a hundred thousand costs a thousand pieces of gold a day. Now there are a hundred thousand law-abiding citizens involved in the prison system; if the government cannot reduce this, I consider that dangerous.

Master Wei Liao

RULERSHIP AND ADMINISTRATION

Maintaining the law, investigating and judging, are duties of administrators; promulgating laws and examining their effects are operations of rulers. Clarifying charges and unifying standards are strategies of administrators and rulers.

Clear rewards and strict punishments are methods of stopping treachery. Examining what to encourage and what to prohibit, keeping to one path, are essentials for government. Effective communication between lower and upper echelons is all-hearing attentiveness.

Knowing what the country has and has not, use the surplus. Knowing others' weaknesses is the essence of strength; knowing others' movements determines stillness. Offices are divided into the civil and the military; these are the two methods of rulership.

Master Wei Liao

ECONOMIC FUNDAMENTALISM

What is there to governing people? They must have food to eat and clothes to wear. So it is a matter of having grain to fill their stomachs and cloth to cover their bodies.

When husbands plow and wives spin, and the peasants do nothing else, then there are surpluses. The men do not engage in painting or sculpture, the women do not embroider fancy sashes. Wooden vessels leak, metal vessels smell; sages cooked in earthenware and ate from earthenware: so if earthen vessels are used there will be no waste.

Master Wei Liao

LAPSE

Now metal and wood vessels naturally do not themselves feel cold, yet people put brocaded coverings over them; horses and oxen naturally eat grasses and drink water, yet they are given beans and millet.

This government has lost its basis; regulations should be established. If the men go out into the fields in the spring and summer and the women make cloth in the fall and winter, then the peasants will not suffer hardship. Now their clothes are inadequate to cover their bodies, dregs and bran won't fill their stomachs; order has been lost.

In ancient times, there were no questions of relative fertility of land or relative diligence of the people. What did the ancients have that people today have lost? If the fields are not completely plowed and the looms are stopped every day, what can be done about cold and hunger? What was practiced in ancient government has lapsed in modern government.

Master Wei Liao

EMPERORS

There are four qualifications for being an emperor: genius, generosity, order, and inviolability.

Master Wei Liao

KINGS OF YORE

According to legends of kings of yore, they commissioned the upright, dismissed the dishonest, gave security to the genial and harmonious, and passed judgments without delay.

Master Wei Liao

TOTAL DEDICATION

Total dedication is a matter of spiritual clarity. Military strategy is a matter of attaining the Way. When what is there is made to seem as if it were not, and what is not there is made to seem as if it were, how can this be trusted?

Master Wei Liao

QUALITIES OF GOVERNMENTS

Consultants today say, "A hundred-league ocean cannot provide even one man with enough to drink, whereas a three-foot spring can quench the thirst of three armies." It seems to me that greediness is born of immoderation, perversity is born of unruliness.

The finest government is by spiritual influence; the next adapts to actualities; the lowest is a matter of not depriving the people of their time and not diminishing the people's possessions. Prohibitions are established by force, awards are established by culture.

Master Wei Liao

STRATEGY AND FORCE

According to the laws of warfare, a thousand men can succeed by strategy, ten thousand men can succeed by force. When you apply strategy to others first, enemies will not clash with you; when you apply force to others first, enemies will not confront you. Therefore in warfare it is important to be first: if you win at this, you will win over others; if you do not win at this, you will not win over others.

Master Wei Liao

AGGRESSIVENESS

Those who know the Way must first take into account the failure of not knowing where to stop; they reject the idea that aggressive action will necessarily have success.

If you seek battle at the drop of a hat, your opponent will then be still, calculating; if you go ahead, your opponent has secured victory.

Therefore the art of warfare dictates that if you follow enemies in pursuit, attacking them on sight, and their leaders do not seem willing to put up a fight, you are losing to their strategy.

Those who have been outmaneuvered are dispirited; those

who are intimidated are vulnerable. When people disappear from the losing side, it is because their army did not have the Way.

When you can proceed deliberately without doubt, then you go ahead. When you can outmaneuver an enemy without fail, then you do it. When you can see clearly and remain out of reach, then you overawe others. This is the consummation of military science.

Master Wei Liao

SUPREMACY WITHOUT COMBAT

If soldiers' talk is indiscreet, they are not serious; if they are bellicose and aggressive without reason, they are bound to crumble. If they attack in bursts and blitzes, their cohorts will be confused. It is necessary to secure dangerous conditions and get rid of problems, resolving them wisely.

Elevate your soldiers' pride in their nation, increase their sense of the importance of their mission, and sharpen their sense of responsiblity. Then enemy nations can be subdued without combat.

Master Wei Liao

SEVERE PENALTIES

Military commanders of more than a thousand people who lose in battle, who surrender when on the defensive, who don't stand their ground but desert their troops, are condemned as thieves of the nation. They are executed, their families are destroyed, their birth records are discarded, their ancestral tombs are dug up, their bones are exposed in public, and their sons and daughters are made state slaves.

Those in command of more than a hundred people who lose in battle, surrender when on the defensive, or abandon their ground and desert their troops are condemned as thieves of the army. They are put to death, their families are destroyed, and their children are enslaved.

If the people are caused to be wary of severe punishments at home, they will think lightly of enemies abroad. Therefore kings of yore clarified regulations at the outset and punished severely and sternly afterward. When punishment is severe, there is internal wariness, and the inwardly wary are outwardly firm.

Master Wei Liao

MUTUAL SURETY SYSTEM

In the organization of the military, five people are a team; the members of the team are surety for each other. Ten people are a squad; the members of the squad are surety for each other. Fifty people make a band; the members of the band are surety for each other. One hundred people make a group; the members of the group are surety for each other.

If a team has members who violate orders or break rules, the others are exempted from punishment if they report it; if they know but don't report it, the whole team is punished. If a squad has members who violate orders or break rules, the others are exempt from punishment if they report it; if they know but do not report it, the whole squad is punished.

If a band has members who violate orders or break rules, the others are exempted from punishment if they report it; if they know but don't report it, the whole band is punished. If a group has members who violate orders or break rules, the others are exempted from punishment if they report it; if they know but don't report it, the whole group is punished.

The officers, from squad leaders to major generals, are all surety for each other: if any violate orders or break rules, those who report it escape punishment, whereas those who know but do not report it are subject to the same punishment.

When the teams and squads are linked and the upper and lower echelons are connected, there is no treachery that is not found out, no wrongdoing that is not reported. Fathers cannot favor their own sons, elder brothers cannot favor their younger brothers. Especially when countrymen lodge together and eat together, how can there be any violation of orders or personal favoritism?

Master Wei Liao

EXTREME TEAMWORK

The rule for binding teams is as follows: Five people make a team, with the same insignia, assigned to a commanding officer. If they lose part of their team but take out a team, these are weighed against each other. If they take out a team without loss, there is an award. If they lose part of their team without taking out a team, they are executed and their families are killed.

If a squad or group chief is lost but a chief is taken out, these are weighed against each other. If a chief is taken out without loss, then there is a reward. If a chief is lost without taking out a chief, the responsible ones are executed and their families are killed, unless they go back into battle and take the head of an enemy chief, which will absolve them.

If a commander is lost in taking out an enemy commander, these are weighed against each other. If an enemy commander is taken out with no losses, there is a reward. If a commander is lost while failing to take out an enemy commander, the responsible ones are charged with desertion.

Master Wei Liao

WARTIME DISCIPLINE

The rule for punishment in wartime is as follows: A squad leader can punish ten people, a group chief can punish a squad leader, a commander of a thousand can punish a chief of a hundred, a commander of ten thousand can punish a commander of a thousand. The generals of the left and right can punish a commander of ten thousand, and a generalissimo can punish anyone.

Master Wei Liao

TIMELINESS

Make decisions as soon as possible, before your enemies do. If your plans are not determined first and your concerns are not quickly resolved, then your maneuvers are uncertain; when hesitation arises, you'll lose out. Therefore an orthodox military operation values preemption, while a surprise military operation values follow-up. Whether to preempt or follow up is a matter of which will overcome the enemy.

Master Wei Liao

THREE HANDICAPS IN WAR

Military commanders of the world who do not know the art of war and who act on their own, taking bold initiatives, are all losers. They do not question questionable things in their operations, they doubt what is certain in their campaigns, they do not slow down and speed up when they need to. These three are handicaps in war.

Master Wei Liao

SENDING THE PEOPLE TO WAR

There is a way to get the people to leave their country to decide issues of life and death, teaching them so that they would go to their death without hesitation. Make sure the defenders are firm, the fighters are combative, interlopers don't act, and liars don't speak. Let orders be carried out without changes, let the troops move without speculation.

Master Wei Liao

TWELVE WAYS OF WINNING VICTORY

There are twelve ways of winning victory, by which it is possible to annex and expand territory and unify a system so that it overpowers everyone:

1. Collective punishment—members of surety teams share mutual responsibility for crimes

2. Area restriction—travel is prohibited so as to net outside interlopers

3. Orderly linking of armored vehicles and infantry

4. Building border fortifications, defended by warriors who will stay at their posts even to their deaths

5. Formation of divisions—left and right watch out for each other, vanguard and rear guard depend on each other, with a wall of armored vehicles for security, to attack and to defend

6. Distinction of signals, so that as the forward lines strive to advance, they are distinguished from the backup such that there is not a disorderly rush in a struggle to be first

7. Insignia to show the order of the lines, so the first and the last are not confused

8. Complete organization, meaning intricate coordination, with everyone having a part

9. Cymbals and drums—effective at arousing and instilling power

10. Arraying armored vehicles—a solid front line, with blinders on the horses

11. Warriors willing to die—talented and strong warriors to man the battle chariots, going back and forth and every which way, coming out with surprise maneuvers to overcome enemies

12. Strong soldiers who man the banners and keep the battalions together, not moving without orders

When these twelve things are taught and established, those who violate the order are not to be pardoned. Then if the army is weak it can be strengthened; a ruler from a lower class can be ennobled; deteriorated order can be revived; disenfranchised people can be attracted; large masses of people can be governed; and large expanses of territory can be maintained. The whole world will be awed, even without aggressive action.

Master Wei Liao

The Art of the Attack

When you attack a country, you must take advantage of its changes. Observe its economy to see its deficits; observe its corruption to see its problems. When those above are perverse and those below are alienated, this is a basis for attacking it.

Master Wei Liao

Targeting Priorities

Where the land is large but the cities small, first take the land; where the cities are large and the land is restricted, first attack the cities. Where the territory is extensive but the population small, cut off the passes; where the territory is small but the population large, build massive earth rings against them.

Master Wei Liao

Causing the People to Thrive

Do not nullify their gains, do not take their time; govern them liberally, facilitate their work, and help them with their problems: then you can command the world.

Master Wei Liao

Morality of Warfare

Weapons are instruments of ill omen; contention is a vice.
Things must have a basis, so kings strike the violent and unruly, based on humaneness and justice.

Warring states try to establish their prestige, resist adversaries, and plot against each other, so they cannot do without
armaments.

Master Wei Liao

Martial and Cultural Functions

Military prowess forms the beams of the army, culture forms
the pillars. Military prowess is outside, culture is inside.
Those who can discern these know who will win and lose.
Culture is the means of seeing what is beneficial and what is
harmful, what is safe and what is dangerous; military prowess
is the means of attacking strong enemies and empowering
offense and defense.

Master Wei Liao

Conscript Armies

Those whose soldiers fear their commanders more than their
enemies will win, while those whose soldiers fear their enemies more than their commanders will lose.

If soldiers show up for duty even a day late, their parents,
wives, and children are all equally guilty. If soldiers go absent
without official leave to return to their homes for even a day,

their parents, wives, and children are equally guilty if they do not arrest them and report them.

Master Wei Liao

UNITY

Unity leads to victory, disunity leads to defeat.

Master Wei Liao

CALMNESS

The calm are orderly; a mad rush leads to chaos.

Master Wei Liao

DESERTION

Soldiers who desert their commanders, and officers who desert their troops, are all to be executed. If an officer in front deserts his troops, an officer in back will be rewarded if he can cut him down and take over command of his troops. Those who do not achieve anything in the army are to be posted at the borders for three years.

Master Wei Liao

ENFORCING PERFORMANCE

When all three armies engage in a major battle, if the top general dies and the commanders of at least five hundred men cannot resist the enemy to the death, they are executed. The

top general's right and left guards at the front are all executed. As for the other soldiers, those who served well in
combat are only demoted one grade, while those who did not
are posted to the frontier for three years.

Master Wei Liao

THREE EXCELLENCES

If regulations stop absence without official leave and prevent
desertion, this is one excellence in an army. If the teams and
squads are linked together and the soldiers and officers assist
each other in battle, this is a second excellence in an army. If
the commanders effectively establish their authority and the
soldiers are disciplined and orderly, signals and orders are
clear and trustworthy, and offense and defense are both competent, this is a third excellence in an army.

Master Wei Liao

MOTIVATION

I have heard that those skilled at employing armies in ancient
times could get half their soldiers to fight to the death; the
next best could get three out of ten to fight to the death; the
least could get one out of ten to fight to the death. Those who
could get half their soldiers to fight to the death can threaten
a whole continent; those who can get three out of ten to fight
to the death can overpower sundry lords. As for those who
can get one out of ten to fight to the death, their orders are
carried out by both officers and soldiers.

Master Wei Liao

COMMON CAUSE

The methods of leadership are to strive to capture the hearts of valiant heroes, reward achievement, and convey intentions to the masses. Therefore anything that is liked in common with the masses can be accomplished, and anything that is disliked in common with the masses can be demolished. Governing the nation and making the home secure are matters of winning people; ruining the nation and destroying the family are due to losing people. All living creatures want to get their will.

Three Strategies

SOFT AND HARD

Military Indicators says, "The soft can overcome the hard, the weak can overcome the strong. Softness is benign, hardness is malignant. The weak are helped by others, the strong are attacked by enemies. There is a place to feign softness, a place to exercise hardness, a place to employ weakness, and a place to apply strength: include all four, and use whichever is best according to the circumstances."

Military Indicators says, "If it can be soft and can be hard, that country will flourish more and more. If it can be weak and can be strong, that country will thrive more and more. If it is only soft or only weak, that country will deteriorate; if it is only hard or only strong, that country will perish."

Three Strategies

THE SUBTLE

It is said, "Everyone craves power, but few can keep the subtle." If you can keep the subtle, you can safeguard your life.

Sages maintain this, acting in response to the triggers of events. When they roll it out, it extends throughout the continent; when they roll it up, it does not even fill a cup. They house it without a house, protect it without walls; they hide it in their hearts, and opponents submit to them.

Three Strategies

ADAPTATION

Change according to adversaries, not taking the initiative but following up on their moves.

Three Strategies

COORDINATION

The way to manage a country is particularly a matter of the elite and the commoners. When you can trust the elite like your own heart and employ the commoners like your four limbs, then no strategy will fail. Wherever you go you will be like limbs and body following each other, bones and joints helping each other; spontaneously following the course of nature, that skill is impeccable.

Three Strategies

CASE BY CASE

Essential to military and civil government is to observe the mentalities of the people in order to distribute the jobs.

The imperiled are to be given security, the fearful are to be humored. Deserters are to be won back, the falsely accused are to be absolved, those with complaints are to be given a hearing.

The lowly are to be elevated, the powerful are to be restrained, the hostile are to be eliminated. The greedy are enriched, the ambitious are employed.

The frightened are sheltered, the crafty are befriended. Slanderers are silenced, critics are tested. Rebels are rejected, the violent are broken down. The self-satisfied are criticized, the submissive are welcomed. The conquered are settled, those who surrender are freed.

Fastnesses taken are held, defiles taken are blocked, inaccessible places taken are garrisoned, cities taken are partitioned, land taken is divided, goods taken are distributed.

Three Strategies

MILITARY METHODS

Enemy movements are watched, preparations are made when enemies approach: when enemies are at ease, they are avoided; when enemies are overbearing, they are waited out; when enemies are violent, they are placated. When enemies are obstreperous, they are treated with justice; when enemies are friendly, they are made allies.

Break them down as they rise up, smash them when there is an opportunity; release statements to mislead them, catch them by dragnet.

Acquire without possessing, dwell without staying, siege without prolonging, stand without taking. The one who does it is yourself, while the ones who take possession are the officers; who knows where the profit is? They become the lords, while you become the emperor, having the cities secure themselves and having the officers make their own exactions.

Three Strategies

Respect and Remuneration

The key to employing an army is to respect order and pay well. If you respect order, intelligent people will come; pay well, and dutiful warriors will readily risk death. So pay the intelligent ungrudgingly and reward achievement promptly; then the lower echelons will pull together and enemy nations will weaken.

The way to employ people is to honor them with ranks and provide for them financially; then knights will come on their own. Treat them with courtesy, inspire them with justice, and the knights will risk death for you.

Three Strategies

Following Orders

Military Indicators says, "The means by which commanders exert authority is by issuing orders. The means by which a battle is won completely is by order in the army. The reason officers will readily fight is that they are following orders. Therefore commanders do not rescind orders, and rewards and penalties are sure as heaven and earth; then they can command others. When officers and soldiers follow orders, then they can cross the borders.

Three Strategies

Going Stale

It is the general who leads the army and maintains its form; it is the troops who seize victory and overcome enemies. Therefore an undisciplined general cannot be employed to su-

45

perintend an army, and unruly troops cannot be employed to attack others. Otherwise they will not succeed in taking the cities they seize or in conquering the towns they surround. Unsuccessful at both, the soldiers will tire, so the general will be isolated and the troops rebellious—then they will be unsure at defense and will flee in combat. This is called a stale army.

When an army goes stale, the general's authority is ineffective; when the general has no authority, then the officers and soldiers slight the rules. When the officers and soldiers slight the rules, then team organization is lost. When team organization is lost, then officers and soldiers run away. When soldiers run away, enemies take advantage. When enemies take advantage, then the army will perish.

Three Strategies

ORGANIZATION AND AUTHORITY

Military Indicators says, "The army has reward on the outside, punishment on the inside. When rewards and punishments are clear, then the authority of the commander is effective. When offices are filled by the right people, then the soldiers obey. When those to whom authority is delegated are intelligent, then enemy nations tremble."

Three Strategies

EFFECTS OF ATTITUDE

Military Indicators says, "Wherever the intelligent go, there are no opponents before them. Therefore officers should be humble, not arrogant; commanders should be cheerful, not anxious; planning should be deeply hidden, not suspicious. If officers are arrogant, their subordinates will not obey them. If commanders are anxious, then those on the inside and outside will not trust each other. If planning is suspected, enemy nations will be aroused."

Three Strategies

THE CHARACTER OF A COMMANDER

Military Indicators says, "A commander is pure, calm, fair, orderly, receptive to advice, listens to complaints, recruits people, samples opinions, knows the customs of nations, can depict the landscape and show the dangers and difficulties, and is able to control the direction of the army. Therefore it is said, 'Commanders should listen to the wisdom of the humane and intelligent, the thoughts of sages and illuminates, the words of peasants, the statements of officials, the things that have to do with flourishing and decline.'"

Three Strategies

ADVICE AND PLANNING

If commanders take their advisers seriously, their plans will be followed. If commanders refuse advice, then valiant heroes will drift away. If plans are not followed, planners will rebel. If good and bad are treated equally, then meritorious administrators will be discouraged.

When the commander is autocratic, subordinates lay all blame on him; when he takes all the credit for himself, his subordinates accomplish little. If he believes slanderers, the troops will become alienated at heart. If he is greedy for money, then conniving cannot be stopped.

Three Strategies

CONFIDENTIALITY, UNITY, AND ALACRITY

Military Indicators says, "The plans of the commander should be confidential; the officers and men should be unified; attacks on enemies should be swift." When the plans of the commander are confidential, then traitors cannot get ideas. When the officers and men are unified, then the army is psychologically cohesive. When attacks on enemies are swift, then they will not have time to prepare against them. If an army has these three things, its plans will not be thwarted.

Three Strategies

LEAKS, GAPS, AND BRIBES

If the commander's plans leak out, then the army will have no power. If outsiders can see inside, then calamity cannot be stopped. When bribe money enters camp, then the dishonest collect. If commanders have these three things, the army is sure to lose.

Three Strategies

FLAWS IN COMMANDERS

If commanders are thoughtless, planners will leave. If commanders lack bravery, officers will be afraid. If commanders move arbitrarily, their armies will not be calm. If commanders take out their anger on others, the whole army will be fearful.

Three Strategies

Psychological and Material Inducements

Military Indicators says, "Where there is tasty bait, there will be hooked fish; where there are serious rewards, there will be men willing to risk their lives. Therefore courtesy is what soldiers take to, rewards are what soldiers risk death for. Invite them to what they resort to, show them what to risk death for, and those who are sought will come. Therefore if you treat them courteously but afterward regret it, soldiers will not stay. If you reward them but afterward regret it, soldiers will not serve. If you do not slack off courtesy and rewards, then soldiers will eagerly risk their lives."

Three Strategies

Knowing the Enemy

Military Indicators says, "Essential to military operations is prior examination of the condition of the enemy. See their stores, calculate their food supplies, figure out their strengths and weaknesses, examine their climate and terrain, search out their voids and gaps."

Three Strategies

Benefits and Popularity

Military Indicators says, "A country that is going to launch a military operation must first grant many benefits; a country that is going to lay a siege must first cherish its people. What enables few to overcome many is appreciation of benefits;

what enables the weaker to overcome the stronger is popularity. Therefore good commanders treat the soldiers no different from the way they treat themselves. Thus, if you can command the three armies as if they were of one mind, your victory can be total."

Three Strategies

OPPRESSION

Military Indicators says, "When superiors act cruelly, subordinates are peremptory and harsh. When taxes and levies are heavy and numerous, punishments are unlimited, and the people prey on each other, that is called a lost nation."

Three Strategies

CORRUPTION

Military Indicators says, "When officials cluster in cliques, each promoting their friends, nominating crooks for appointments, suppressing and thwarting the good and the intelligent, turning their backs on the public for the sake of their own private interests, slandering their colleagues, this is called a source of disorder."

Three Strategies

POWERFUL CLANS

Military Indicators says, "When powerful clans gather crafty villains, they become distinguished without having any official rank, making everyone tremble at their power. Like entangling vines, they get others indebted to them by selective favors; usurping the authority of those in office, they violate and abuse the common people. The country is in an uproar, but the government ministers conceal it and do not report it. This is called a root of disorder."

Three Strategies

DAMAGE AND HARM

Military Indicators says, "When there are disproportionately many officials in comparison with the size of the populace, or the noble and the base are on a par, or the strong victimize the weak, or no one follows controls, this affects the leadership, and the nation suffers consequent damage."

Military Indicators says, "When the good are recognized as good but are not promoted, the evil are recognized as evil but are not dismissed, the wise are obscured while the corrupt are in office, the nation suffers harm from that."

Three Strategies

SUBTLE STRATEGY

Military Indicators says, "Use intelligence, use bravery, use greed, use folly. Intellectuals like to establish their merit, the brave like to carry out their ambitions, the greedy seek profit, the foolish are unfazed by the risk of death. To use them according to their true conditions is the subtle strategy of warfare."

Three Strategies

THE EVOLUTION OF GOVERNMENT

The Three August Ones made no speeches, but their influence circulated everywhere, so the world had nowhere to attribute the merit.

As for the emperors, they emulated heaven and followed the laws of the earth; they made speeches and gave orders, so the world became very peaceful. The leaders and administrators deferred the merit to each other, so while their influence prevailed everywhere, the common people did not know why it was so. Therefore they employed administrators effectively without the need for ceremonies or prizes, getting along fine without impediment.

As for the kings, they governed people by means of the Way, conquering their hearts and winning their minds, establishing regulations to guard against corruption. Local leaders from all over convened, and tribute to the kings was kept up. Though they had military preparations, they had no warfare. The rulers were not suspicious of the administrators, and the administrators were not suspicious of the rulers. The country was stable, the ruler secure, the administrators retired when proper. They too could get along fine, without obstruction.

As for the hegemons, they governed men by means of strategy, mustered men by means of confidence, and employed men by means of awards. When confidence deteriorated, the men drifted away; when awards were lacking, the men would not obey orders.

Three Strategies

INTEGRITY AND DIGNITY

Leaders must have integrity, for if they lack integrity their administators will defy them. Leaders must have dignity, for if they lack dignity they will lose their authority.

Three Strategies

FASCISM

Military Configurations says, "Do not let orators extol the virtues of adversaries, lest they confuse the masses. Do not put philanthropists in charge of finances, because they will give away a lot and win the adherence of the lower classes."

Three Strategies

CONSCIENCE

Military Configurations says, "You cannot employ righteous people just by money. Righteous men will not risk death for the inhumane, wise people will not devise strategies for ignorant rulers."

Three Strategies

SUBTERFUGE AND SECRECY

When sage kings rule the world, they observe flourishing and decline, assess gain and loss, and legislate accordingly. Therefore local lords have one army, regional overlords have three armies, and the emperor has six armies.

When society is chaotic, rebellion arises, government benefits dry up, and factions form and attack each other. If their merits are similar and their powers comparable, so they cannot overthrow each other, that is the time to capture the hearts and minds of heroic stalwarts, share the likes and dislikes of the masses, and then after that apply tactical adaptations.

So without strategy there is no way to settle confusion and doubt; if not for subterfuge and surprise there is no way to defeat treachery and stop enemies; without secret planning there is no way to achieve success.

Three Strategies

THE STRATEGY OF HEGEMONS

Once an army has been assembled, it cannot be dispersed abruptly; once authority has been granted, it cannot be transferred abruptly. Demobilizing an army is a life-and-death situation—weaken them with positions, undermine them with land grants: this is called the strategy of hegemons.

Three Strategies

THREE LEVELS OF STRATEGY

Sages emulate heaven, the wise emulate earth, the knowledgeable emulate ancients. Therefore three levels of strategy were devised for deteriorating societies.

Higher strategy establishes honors and awards, distinguishes frauds from stalwarts, clarifies the causes of victory and defeat, success and failure.

Intermediate strategy differentiates qualities and behaviors and analyzes strategic adaptations.

Lower strategy sets forth normative virtues, examines safety and danger, and clarifies the error of thwarting the wise.

So if leaders have a profound understanding of higher strategy, they are able to appoint the wise and capture enemies.

If they have a profound understanding of intermediate strategy, they can command generals and rule the troops.

If they have a profound understanding of lower strategy, they can understand the sources of flourishing and decline, and comprehend the principles of governing a nation.

If administrators have a deep understanding of intermediate strategy, they can complete their work and preserve themselves.

Three Strategies

BENEVOLENCE

Those who can help the world when in danger can thus establish peace in the world. Those who can eliminate the world's anxieties can thus experience the world's pleasures. Those who can save the world from calamity can thus obtain the blessings of the world.

So if your benevolence extends to the people, then wise men will take to you; if your benevolence reaches all creatures, then sages will take to you. If wise men take to you, your country will be strong; if sages take to you, the whole world will be united.

Seek wise men by integrity, bring sages by the Way. When wise men leave, then a country weakens; when sages leave, a country loses social cohesion. Weakness borders on peril; lack of social cohesion is a foresign of ruin.

Three Strategies

MASTERY OF BODY AND MIND

Government by the intelligent masters people physically; government by sages masters people mentally. By mastery of the body, it is possible to plan beginnings; by mastery of the mind, it is possible to guarantee ends.

Mastering the body is done by ritual, mastering the mind is done by enjoyment. Enjoyment does not mean music: it means people enjoy their homes, it means people enjoy their families, it means people enjoy their jobs, it means people enjoy their cities, it means people enjoy their social order, it means people enjoy their virtues.

Three Strategies

TEACHING OTHERS

Those who try to teach others while ignoring themselves are opposed. Those who teach others after having rectified themselves are obeyed. Opposition beckons disorder, obedience is key to order.

Three Strategies

PLANNING, RELAXATION, AND SECURITY

If you leave aside the near at hand and plan for the remote, you will toil without success; if you leave aside the remote and plan for the near at hand, you will be at ease and yet will succeed.

A relaxed government has many loyal administrators; a burdensome government has many resentful people. Therefore it is said that those who strive to expand territory become destitute, while those who strive to expand benevolence become strong.

Those who can keep what they have are secure, while those who crave what others have are destroyed. The afflictions caused by destructive policies are felt for generations. Artificially create excessive regulation, and even if it works it will eventually fail.

Three Strategies

VALUES

The Way, virtue, humaneness, justice, courtesy—these five are one body. The Way is for people to tread, virtue is for people to attain, humaneness attracts people, justice is what is right for people, courtesy is what people embody; it will not do to lack even one of these.

Rising early and retiring late is a form of courtesy; striking down brigands and wreaking vengeance on enemies is the decisiveness of justice; feeling pity is an expression of humaneness; self-mastery and winning others are routes of virtue; and causing people to be equal, not out of place, is the influence of the Way.

Three Strategies

DIRECTIVES, ORDERS, AND POLICIES

What comes from the ruler to the administrators is called a directive; in written form it is called an order; in action it is called a policy. If a directive is mistaken, the order is ineffective. If the order is ineffective, the policy is not right. If the policy is not right, the Way does not go through. If the Way does not go through, then corrupt administrators prevail. If corrupt administrators prevail, then the prestige and authority of the ruler are injured.

Three Strategies

NEAR AND FAR

Welcome the wise from a thousand miles away, and the road is far; bring on the dishonest, and the road is near. In this sense enlightened rulers leave the near aside and take the far; then they can complete their work and elevate people, while subordinates put forth all their effort.

Three Strategies

GOOD AND BAD

Ignore one good, and all good deteriorates; reward one evil, and myriad evils come. When the good is fostered and the bad is punished, then the country is secure and all good arrives.

Three Strategies

UNCERTAINTY AND CONFUSION

When the masses are uncertain, there is no stabilizing the nation; when the masses are confused, there is no governing the populace. When uncertainties are settled and confusion removed, then the country can be secure.

Three Strategies

EQUALITY BY PURITY

When one order is opposed, a hundred orders are neglected. When one evil is perpetrated, a hundred evils accumulate. So when good is done to docile people and ill is visited upon vicious people, then order prevails without resentment. If you govern bitter people with bitterness, that is called violating nature. If you govern hostile people with hostility, calamity will be inevitable. Govern the people so as to make them equal, effecting equality by purity, and the people will find their places and the world will be at peace.

Three Strategies

PURE PEOPLE

When the rebellious are honored and the greedy are rich, even a sage king could not bring about order. When the rebellious are punished and the greedy are restrained, then order prevails and myriad evils vanish.

Pure people cannot be won by ranks and salaries; just people cannot be threatened by intimidation or imprisonment. Therefore when enlightened rulers seek wise people, they must attract them by considering their motivations. To attract pure people, cultivate your courtesy. To attract just people, cultivate the Way. Then people can be attracted and honor can be preserved.

Three Strategies

SAGACIOUS GENTLEMEN

Sagacious gentlemen understand the sources of flourishing and decline, comprehend the beginnings of success and failure, understand the triggers of order and chaos, and know the timing of actions. Even if they are in straits, they will not occupy the throne of a moribund nation, and even if they are poor, they will not live off a stipend from a disorderly nation. Those who anonymously embrace the Way go into action when the time comes.

Three Strategies

INSIDERS AND OUTSIDERS

When wise ministers are on the inside, corrupt ministers are kept out. When corrupt ministers are on the inside, then wise ministers die out. When inside and outside lose their proper places, calamity and disorder go on for generations.

Three Strategies

PRETENDERS AND PROXIES

When high-ranking administrators pretend to rulership, the treacherous gather. When ministers are as respected as rulers, then hierarchy is obscured. When rulers are in the positions of ministers, the hierarchy loses its order.

Three Strategies

PROMOTING THE WISE

For those who injure the wise, troubles continue for three generations. Those who obscure the wise personally suffer harm from that. Those who envy the wise are not completely reputable. For those who promote the wise, blessings extend to their descendants. Therefore if rulers are intent on promoting the wise, they will get a good reputation.

Three Strategies

COHESION

If you harm a hundred in profiting one individual, the people will leave; if you harm ten thousand to profit one individual, the country will lose cohesion. If you profit a hundred by getting rid of one individual, people will appreciate the favor.

If you profit ten thousand by getting rid of one individual, social order will not be disrupted.

Three Strategies

THE WAY OF ANCIENT SAGES

King Wen asked Taigong, "May I hear where the Way of ancient sages stops and where it starts?"

Taigong said, "To be indolent when seeing good to be done, to be hesitant when the time arrives, to abide what is known to be wrong—these are where the Way stops.

"To be soft and calm, respectful and serious, strong yet flexible, tolerant yet firm—these four are where the Way starts. So when your sense of justice overcomes desire, you flourish; when desire overcomes your sense of justice, you perish. When seriousness overcomes indolence, that is auspicious; when indolence overcomes seriousness, that is destructive."

Six Strategies

WEALTH AND WELFARE

Rulers must pursue wealth, because without wealth they have no way to practice benevolence; if they are not generous, they have no way to unite clansmen. Those who alienate clansmen come to harm; those who lose the masses come to ruin. Do not lend others sharp instruments; if you lend others sharp instruments you will be harmed by others and not live out your life.

Six Strategies

BENEVOLENCE AND DUTY

King Wen asked, "What are benevolence and duty?"

Taigong said, "Respect the masses, unify your clansmen. If you respect the masses, they will be harmonious; if you unify your clansmen, they will be joyful. These are the outlines of benvolence and duty.

"Don't let anyone take away your dignity. Use your insight, follow normalcy. Those who are obedient should be employed rewardingly; those who are disruptive should be stopped powerfully. Honor these without doubt, and the whole land will peacefully submit."

Six Strategies

DEMAND AND SUPPLY

When the land is orderly, humane sages hide; when the land is chaotic, humane sages rise.

Six Strategies

LEADERSHIP AND QUALITY OF LIFE

King Wen asked Taigong, "The world is complex. Now waxing, now waning, now orderly, now chaotic—why is it like this? Is it because of differences in the quality of leadership? Is it a natural result of changes in the times?"

Taigong said, "If the leadership is unworthy, a nation is perilous and its people unruly. If the leadership is wise, a nation is peaceful and its people are orderly. Calamity and fortune depend on the leadership, not on the times."

Six Strategies

DEMEANOR

Be calm and serene, gentle and moderate. Be generous, not contentious; be openhearted and even-minded. Treat people correctly.

Six Strategies

ARBITRARY APPROVAL

Do not give arbitrary approval, yet do not refuse out of mere contrariness. Arbitrary approval means loss of discipline, while refusal means shutting off.

Six Strategies

BASES OF DEMOCRACY

Look with the eyes of the whole land, and there is nothing you will not see. Listen with the ears of the whole land, and there is nothing you will not hear. Think with the minds of the whole land, and there will be nothing you do not know.

Six Strategies

SIX ELEMENTS OF DEFENSE

There are six elements of defense: (1) humanity, (2) duty, (3) loyalty, (4) trustworthiness, (5) courage, (6) strategy.

There are ways to choose people for these six elements of defense.

1. Enrich them and see if they refrain from misconduct. (This proves humanity.)
2. Ennoble them and see if they refrain from hauteur. (This proves duty.)
3. Give them responsibilities and see if they refrain from autocratic behavior. (This proves loyalty.)
4. Employ them and see if they refrain from deceit. (This proves trustworthiness.)
5. Endanger them and see if they are unafraid. (This proves courage.)
6. Burden them and see if they are unflagging. (This proves strategy.)

Six Strategies

How to Preserve Territory

Do not alienate relatives.
Do not neglect the masses.
Treat associates well.
Keep the four quarters under control.
Do not lend national authority to another.
Do not take from the have-nots to give more to the haves.
Do not neglect fundamentals to deal with trivia.

Six Strategies

Six Parasites

1. Officials who build huge mansions and estates and pass their time in entertainment
2. Workers who don't work but go around getting into others' business, disrupting social order

3. Officials who form cliques that obscure the good and the wise and thwart the enlightened
4. Ambitious officers who independently communicate with leaders of other groups, without deference to their own leaders
5. Executives who disregard rank, look down on teamwork, and are unwilling to go to trouble for employers
6. Strong factions who overpower the weak and resourceless

Six Strategies

Seven Harmful Things

1. Those who are lacking in intelligent tactical strategy but are pugnacious and combative out of ambition for reward and titles should not be made into commanders.
2. Self-contradicting opportunists and pretenders who obscure the good and elevate the bad should not be made into planners.
3. Those who put on the appearance of austerity and desirelessness in order to get something should not be approached.
4. Those who pretend to be eccentric intellectuals, putting on airs and looking upon the world with aloof contempt, should not be favored.
5. The dishonest and unscrupulous who seek office and entitlement by flattery and unfair means, who display bravery out of greed for emolument, who act opportunistically without consideration of the big picture, who persuade leaders with tall tales and empty talk, should not be employed.
6. Compromising primary production by needless luxury should be prohibited.

7. Use of supposed occult arts and superstitious practices to bewilder decent people should be stopped.

Six Strategies

Duties

People who do not do their best are not my people.

Warriors who are not truthful and trustworthy are not my warriors.

Ministers who do not admonish faithfully are not my ministers.

Officials who do not care for the people with fairness and integrity are not my officials.

Administrators who cannot enrich the country, strengthen the military, harmonize the negative and the positive, stabilize the national government, keep all the ministers honest, define titles and realities, clarify rewards and punishments, and bring happiness to the common people are not my administrators.

Six Strategies

The Way of the Dragon

The way of rulership is like the head of a dragon, dwelling on high and gazing afar, looking deeply and listening closely. It shows its form but hides its feelings. As high as the sky, it cannot be comprehended; as deep as the abyss, it cannot be fathomed.

Six Strategies

ANGER

If you do not get angry when it is appropriate to be angered, treacherous ministers will act. If you do not execute those who should be executed, major rebellions will break out. If the power of the military cannot be mobilized, enemy nations are strong.

Six Strategies

FALSE REPUTATION

King Wen asked Taigong, "If the leadership tries to promote the worthy but cannot get effective results, why is that?"

Taigong said, "Promoting the worthy without letting them work—that is, to have the reputation of promoting the worthy but in reality not using them."

King Wen asked, "Where is the fault?"

Taigong said, "It is in the leadership's going on the basis of vulgar popularity or social recommendation and not finding really worthy people."

King Wen asked, "How is this?"

Taigong said, "If the leadership considers popular approval to be worthy and unpopularity to be unworthy, then those with many partisans get ahead, while those with few partisans fall behind. If so, then crooks will be everywhere, obscuring the worthy; loyal administrators will be executed for no crime, while treacherous bureaucrats will assume rank by means of false reputations. Thus social disorder increases, so the nation cannot avoid peril and perdition."

Six Strategies

Appointing the Worthy

King Wen asked Taigong, "How are the worthy appointed?"

Taigong said, "Military commanders and civilian administrators each have their own separate jobs, so people are nominated individually for specific offices. Examine the reality of the office in respect to its title, choose people with the appropriate talents, taking their abilities into consideration, making the realities fit the titles."

Six Strategies

Awards and Punishments

King Wen asked, "Awards are for encouragement, punishments are for admonition. I want to reward one in such a way as to encourage a hundred, and punish one in such a way as to admonish everyone—how can I do that?"

Taigong said, "Rewards should be reliable, penalties should be inevitable. When rewards are reliable and penalties are inevitable within the range of seeing and hearing, then those out of range of seeing and hearing will be unknowingly affected."

Six Strategies

The Way of Warfare

King Wen asked Taigong, "What is the way of warfare?"

Taigong said, "Nothing in the way of warfare is more important than unity. Unity means the ability to come and go independently. The Yellow Emperor said, 'Unity is approaching the Way, drawing near to the uncanny. Its use is in opportunity, its manifestation is in formation and momentum; its fulfillment is a matter of leadership.' Therefore sage kings called weapons instruments of ill omen, to be used only when unavoidable."

Six Strategies

SWIFT RESPONSE

King Wu asked Taigong, "If enemies find out our true conditions and know our plans, what should we do about it?"

Taigong said, "The art of military victory is to intimately examine enemies' workings and quickly take advantage of them, and quickly attack where they do not expect it."

Six Strategies

RECIPROCITY

The world opens up to those who profit the world; the world closes down to those who harm the world. The world is not one individual's world, it is the world's world.

Those who would take the world are like chasing wild animals, with everyone wanting a share of the meat. Those who cross over a river in the same boat share the same advantage if they make it across, and they share the same harm if they fail: therefore everyone has a reason to facilitate the crossing, and none will stop it.

Those who do not take from the people are those who take the people; those who do not take from the nation are those who take the nation; those who do not take from the world are those who take the world.

The people help those who do not take from the people; a

nation helps those who do not take from the nation; the world helps those who do not take from the world.

Six Strategies

SUBTLETIES OF STRATEGY

The Way is a matter of invisibility, business is a matter of confidentiality, victory is a matter of inscrutability. This is very subtle.

Six Strategies

SYMPTOMS OF SICKNESS

When many voices confuse each other, disorder goes on and on, and sexual debauchery is unlimited, these are signs of a moribund nation. If we see weeds and reeds choking the valleys in the countryside, if we see the crooked prevailing over the honest among the populace, if we see cruelty and viciousness in officials, if the legal system is corrupt and the leadership is not aware of it, that is the time when a nation is perishing.

Six Strategies

EFFICIENCY

Where government works effectively, no one is aware of its influence; when the time is the present, no one is aware of its movement.

Six Strategies

PEOPLE

People are like flowing water: obstruct them and they stagnate, open channels for them and they move, calm them and they become purified.

Six Strategies

NONVIOLENT ATTACK

King Wen asked Taigong, "What are the methods of nonviolent attack?"

Taigong said, "There are twelve elements of nonviolent attack:

1. "Go along with what enemies like, to get them to indulge their will. They will get conceited, there will surely be misconduct—if you can make use of this, you will be able to get rid of them.
2. "Get close to those they love, in order to divide their influence. When a people is divided in mind, their loyalty inevitably deteriorates. When there are no loyal ministers at court, the nation is surely in peril.
3. "Secretly bribe their associates to get informaton in great depth. Where information leaks out from insiders, that country is going to have problems.
4. "Encourage them in debauchery and hedonism, to extend their desires. Ply them with pearls and jade, delight them with beautiful women. Speak to them humbly and listen fawningly, following their directions and agreeing, until they would no longer fight with you; then the scene is set for treachery.

5. "Honor their loyal ministers but without giving them much. Keep their ambassadors but without listening to their business; have them replaced quickly, sending them off with something true to gain friendship and trust, so that the rulers will ally with you. If you can honor them, their country can be plotted against.

6. "Buy off insiders at court and alienate those in the field: when talented ministers serve the interests of other countries and enemy nations invade, rare is the state that does not perish.

7. "To control their minds, bribe them richly while buying the loyalty and affection of their associates, secretly showing them advantages, inducing them to slight their work, thus building up deficiencies.

8. "Bribe them with valuables, using this to conspire with them in planning strategies that will profit them. If you profit them, they will trust you; this is called rapprochement. When rapprochement builds up, you can exploit them. When the state is subject to external influence, its land will be much reduced.

9. "Honor them with praise and do not criticize their persons. Appear to regard them as very powerful, and go along with them, assuring them of your sincerity. Flatter and glorify them so they put on airs, and their country will become dishonest.

10. "Humble yourself to them so they are sure you are sincere, in order to win their hearts; do things as they wish, as if you were family. Once you have won them over, subtly take them in; when the time comes, it will be as if heaven had destroyed them.

11. "Cloister them strategically. All human subjects value wealth and status and hate death and disaster. Present prospects of high rank while stealthily handing out valuables to buy off their stalwarts. Build up abundant

surpluses within while outwardly seeming poor. Covertly bring in knowledgeable people and have them formulate strategies; bring in brave warriors and elevate their spirits; satisfy them with riches and rank, and their numbers will continue to increase. Once you have cohorts, that means you can cloister others; if they have states but are cloistered, how can they maintain their states?

12. "Cultivate their unruly ministers to mislead them, provide them with beautiful women and licentious music to befuddle them, send them hounds and horses for recreation, seduce them by always conceding great power to them, and watch for the chance to plot against them with the rest of the world."

Six Strategies

GOVERNING THE WORLD

When your mettle covers the world, then you can embrace the world; when your faithfulness covers the world, then you can bind the world to a compact. When your humaneness covers the world, then you can take the world to heart. When your generosity covers the world, then you can preserve the world. When your conduct of affairs is not hesitant or doubtful, then celestial movements cannot alter it, changes in the times cannot shift it. When these six elements are all present, then you can govern the world.

Six Strategies

FAIR TRADE

The world opens up to those who benefit the world, and the world closes down on those who harm the world. The world rewards those who put the world first, and the world destroys those who kill the world. The world communicates with those who understand the world; the world opposes those who frustrate the world. The world relies on those who give security to the world; the world annihilates those who endanger the world.

Six Strategies

Playing Hardball

How to attack the strong, cause disaffection within an enemy camp, and cause their following to dissolve:

Use them, be careful of your strategy, and use money.

To attack the strong, it is necessary to strengthen them even more, until they get overextended: those who are too strong must break, those who are overextended must have gaps. Attack strength by means of strength, cause disaffection by means of affection, dissolve a group by means of the group.

In general, the way of strategy values comprehensiveness and secrecy. Propose things to them, tease them with prospects of gain, and contentiousness is sure to arise. If you want to alienate their familiars, use their loved ones and favorites: offer them what they desire, show them how they can profit, and use this to estrange them, so they cannot get their will. In the glee of their greed for gain, residual doubts about you will cease.

In general, the way to attack is to first make sure to block off their information; then attack their power, destroy their major cities, and get rid of things that harm their people. Debauch them with sex, bait them with favors, fatten them with feasts, entertain them with music. Once you have alienated their familiars, you can surely distance them from their people. Without letting them know your strategy, take them in by being supportive. When no one is aware of your intentions, then you can succeed.

Six Strategies

DOMESTICATING PEOPLE

There must be no stinting in generosity to the people. People are like oxen and horses: if you feed them repeatedly, they will follow you with affection.

Six Strategies

CAPACITIES OF COMMANDERS

Commanders should have five capacities: courage, intelligence, benevolence, trustworthiness, loyalty.

The courageous cannot be violated.

The intelligent cannot be thrown into confusion.

The benevolent are humanistic.

The trustworthy do not deceive people.

The loyal have no duplicity.

Six Strategies

EXCESSES IN COMMANDERS

There are ten excesses in the ways of commanders:

1. There are those who are so bold they slight death.
2. There are those who rush so much their minds are speedy.

3. There are those who are so greedy they are inclined to
   profiteering.
4. There are those who are so kindly they cannot bear to
   let people get hurt.
5. There are those who are so intelligent they are timid.
6. There are those who are so trusting they like to trust
   others.
7. There are those who are so puritanical they don't care
   for other people.
8. There are those who are so intelligent they are psychologically easygoing.
9. There are those who are so strong they act on their
   own initiative.
10. There are those who are so soft they like to delegate
    authority to others.

Those who are so bold they slight death can be induced to
expose themselves to violence.

Those who rush so much their minds are speedy can be
waited out.

Those who are so greedy they are inclined to profiteering
can be bribed.

Those who are so kindly they cannot bear to let people get
hurt can be put to a lot of trouble.

Those who are so intelligent they are timid can be
squeezed.

Those who are so trusting they like to trust others can be
fooled.

Those who are so puritanical they don't care for other people can be degraded.

Those who are so intelligent they are psychologically easygoing are vulnerable to sudden assault.

Those who are so strong they act on their own initiative
are vulnerable to preoccupation.

Those who are so soft they like to delegate authority to others can be deceived.

Six Strategies

WARFARE

Warfare is a major affair for a nation, leading to survival or destruction, and its direction is up to the general. The general is a helper of the nation, so it is imperative to be particular when appointing a general. So it is said that both sides don't win at war; neither do both lose: if a military force goes beyond the borders, if it hasn't overthrown an enemy state, there will be a general with a broken army.

Six Strategies

APPEARANCE AND REALITY

Outward appearances may not correspond to inner realities in fifteen ways:

1. There are those who are smart but are unworthy.
2. There are those who are nice but are thieving.
3. There are those who put on an appearance of respect while being contemptuous at heart.
4. There are those who are outwardly modest but inwardly insincere.
5. There are those who are energetic and spirited but without real sense.
6. There are those who are very serious yet are insincere.

7. There are those who like strategizing but lack decisiveness.

8. There are those who seem bold but lack ability.

9. There are those who seem honest but are unreliable.

10. There are those who seem unstable but are actually loyal and solid.

11. There are those who use subterfuge and agitation but get effective results.

12. There are those who are outwardly courageous but inwardly cowardly.

13. There are those who are very proper and mannerly but actually slight people.

14. There are those who are stern and severe yet calm and guileless.

15. There are those who seem void of forcefulness and physically inferior yet when they go forth never fail to reach their objective and never fail to succeed.

What the whole world looks down upon is valued by sages. What ordinary people do not know, you cannot even begin to see unless you are very clear and lucid.

These distinctions are known by means of eight tests:

1. Question people verbally to observe their expression.

2. Cross-examine them thoroughly to observe their versatility.

3. Spy on them to see whether they are truthful.

4. Question them in revealing ways to observe their integrity.

5. Put them in charge of funds to see if they're honest.

6. Test them with sex to see if they're chaste.

7. Warn them of trouble to see if they're brave.

8. Intoxicate them with alcohol to see how they behave.

If you do all these things, the worthy and unworthy will be distinct.

Six Strategies

PENALTIES AND PRIZES

A commander establishes his authority by executing people of high status and establishes his intelligence by rewarding people of low status; he makes prohibitions and orders effective by thoroughness.

Therefore if there is one man whose execution would make the armed forces all tremble, he executes him; if there is one man whose reward would make myriad men happy, he rewards him. Executions are most effective when big people are executed; rewards are most effective when little people are rewarded.

When even high-ranking, important ministers in office can be executed, then penalties reach all the way to the top echelons. When even oxherds, horse grooms, and stable workers can be rewarded, then awards reach all the way to the lower echelons. When penalties reach all the way up and prizes reach all the way down, the commander's authority is effective.

If the armed forces do not listen when one man is executed, if myriad people do not pay attention when one man is executed, if the masses are not afraid when one man is executed, then even if he executes many men the commander is not taken seriously.

When the armed forces are not happy when one man is enfeoffed, when myriad people are not delighted when one man is rewarded, this means that rewards are ineffective; the rewards are valuing the incapable. Under these conditions, the armies will not work for the commander; this is how to lose the people.

Six Strategies

Top Talent

Those who are skilled at eliminating troubles manage them before they arise; those who are skilled at overcoming enemies prevail in formlessness. The highest warfare does not involve combat; therefore those who fight for victory on fronts of naked blades are not good commanders; those who set up defenses after already having lost are not top sages. Those whose wisdom is average are not leaders of nations; those whose skills are average are not artisans of nations.

Six Strategies

Certainty and Secrecy

No concern is greater than certain victory. No function is greater than inscrutable silence. No action is greater than the unexpected. No strategy is greater than the unknown.

Six Strategies

Halving the Work

Sure winners battle only after seeing weakness in an enemy; this halves the work and doubles the effect.

Six Strategies

ADVANTAGE AND TIMING

Those who are skilled in warfare sit tight, unruffled: when they see victory, they rise; if not, they desist. Therefore it is said, "Don't be afraid, don't be hesitant."

Nothing is more damaging to military operations than hesitation; nothing is more harmful to armed forces than doubt. The skilled do not miss the opportunity when they see an advantage; when the right time comes, they do not doubt.

If you lose the advantage and miss the right timing, you will have trouble. Therefore the wise pursue advantage and timing relentlessly; the skilful do not hesitate once they have made a decision.

Six Strategies

FORESIGHT

How does one know whether an enemy is strong or weak, and foresee the signs of victory and defeat before entering into combat?

Of the signs of victory and defeat, the psychological ones show first. Enlightened commanders observe them; the proof is in the people. Carefully watch enemies' comings and goings, observe their movements and their repose, see what the officers and soldiers are saying, if their talk is pessimistic or optimistic.

Six Strategies

SIGNS OF STRENGTH AND WEAKNESS

When the armed forces are happy, the officers and soldiers respect the rules and honor the directives of their commander, finding mutual joy in smashing enemies, inspiring each other with bravery and ferocity, honoring each other for awesome martial prowess; these are signs of strength.

If the armed forces repeatedly fret, the officers and soldiers are unkempt, they scare each other with talk about the enemy, they talk about unfavorable possibilities, they snoop and gossip no end, myriad mouths confusing each other, with no fear of rules or orders and no respect for the commander, these are signs of weakness.

Six Strategies

HUMANITY AND JUSTICE

In ancient times, humaneness was considered basic and government by justice was considered standard. When the standard did not achieve its aim, then strategy was formulated. Strategy emerges in conflict; it does not come from mediators. Therefore, if killing some individuals secures peace for the people, then killing them is acceptable; if attacking a state would be good for its populace, then attacking it is acceptable. If it is possible to stop war by waging war, then even warfare is acceptable.

The Warrior Code of the Charioteers

LOVE AND AWE

The humane are beloved, the just are appreciated, the wise are relied upon, the brave are emulated, the trustworthy are trusted. To gain the love of one's own people is means of defense; to win the awe of others is means of waging war.

The Warrior Code of the Charioteers

CARING FOR BOTH SIDES

The way of war is to avoid violating the season and distressing the people, thus caring for one's own populace; to avoid attacking when there is confusion and taking advantage of misfortune, caring for the populace of the adversary; and to avoid mobilizing the military in winter or summer, so as to care for the population on both sides.

The Warrior Code of the Charioteers

MILITARISM AND DEFENSE

Even if a state is big, if it is militaristic it will perish. But even if the world is at peace, if it forgets about war it is in peril.

The Warrior Code of the Charioteers

PREPAREDNESS

Once the land is pacified, the emperor relaxes yet still practices hunting in spring and autumn, while the local leaders organize troops in spring and train militias in autumn. By this means they do not forget about warfare.

The Warrior Code of the Charioteers

ETHICS OF ANCIENT WARRIORS

In ancient times, warriors did not chase fleeing soldiers more than a hundred paces and did not pursue a retreating army more than three marches; thus they showed their chivalry.

They did not overtax the incapable and were merciful to the wounded and sick; thus they showed their humaneness.

They let battalions form before attacking them; thus they showed their fairness.

They fought for principle, not for profit; thus they showed their justice.

They granted amnesty to those who surrendered; thus they showed their courage.

They knew how things begin and how they turn out; thus they showed their intelligence.

These six virtues were taught together at appropriate times as a means of uniting the people. This is the policy of time immemorial.

The Warrior Code of the Charioteers

GOVERNMENT BY ENLIGHTENED VIRTUE

The government of ancient kings followed the laws of nature, built upon the advantages of earth, and assigned the virtuous among the people to offices; they kept things in order by accurate definition, set up states and divided duties, paying salaries according to rank. Local leaders were gladly sympathetic, while foreign powers paid tribute. Punishments disappeared and war ceased. This is government by enlightened virtue.

The Warrior Code of the Charioteers

THE GOVERNMENT OF WISE KINGS

Next best to government by enlightened virtue is the government of wise kings, who established ritual, music, and law, then created penalties and mobilized soldiery to attack the unjust.

Going on fact-finding tours, examining regional ways, they assembled local leaders and considered their differences. If any had forfeited their mandate, disturbing normalcy, rejecting morality, opposing nature, and threatening a meritorious leader, wise kings would announce it to all the local chieftains, making the crime clearly known, declaring it even to God on high, and to the Sun, Moon, stars, and planets.

Praying to the spirits of the earth and seas, mountains and local shrines, they appealed to their ancestors. Only after that would the prime ministers draft troops from the local chieftains.

The Warrior Code of the Charioteers

COMMANDS TO THE TROOPS OF AN INVADING ARMY

"When you enter the territory of an offender, let there be no desecration of sacred shrines, no hunting in the fields, no destruction of infrastructure, no burning residential areas, no deforestation, no confiscation of domestic animals, grains, or machinery. When you see the old and the young, escort them to safety and do not let them get hurt; and even if you meet able-bodied men, do not attack them if they do not engage you in confrontation. If you wound opponents, give them medical treatment and send them home."

When the offender has been executed, the central and local authorities restructure the state, nominating good people to establish enlightened leadership, restoring social order.

The Warrior Code of the Cavaliers

CENTRAL AND LOCAL AUTHORITY (1)

Central authority has six ways of governing local leaders: (1) circumscribing the territories of local leaders, (2) equalizing local leaders by government policy, (3) winning the goodwill of local leaders by courtesy and trustworthiness, (4) pleasing local leaders by employing the talented, (5) using strategists to bind local leaders, and (6) using armaments to overpower local leaders. Sharing their troubles as well as their gains to unite local leaders, harmonize local leaders through closeness with the small and service to the great.

The Warrior Code of the Cavaliers

CENTRAL AND LOCAL AUTHORITY (2)

There are nine reasons for central authorities to assemble local leaders and issue interdictions.

1. Those who take advantage of the weak and violate the rights of minorities are to have their territories reduced.
2. Those who persecute the good and harm the populace are to be struck down.
3. Those who are cruel in their own domains and contemptuous of others are to be imprisoned.
4. Those whose fields are overgrown and populace scattered are to have their territory cut down.
5. Those who take advantage of fastnesses to be rebellious are to be invaded.
6. Those who kill their parents are to be corrected.
7. Those who depose or assassinate their rulers are to be eliminated.

8. Those who disobey orders and are contemptuous of the government are to be terminated.

9. Those who are unruly abroad and at home, behaving like animals, are to be exterminated.

The Warrior Code of the Cavaliers

DUTIES

The duty of emperors is to derive laws purely from nature and consider the examples of past sages.

The duty of ordinary people is to serve their parents and be correct in respect to their leaders and elders.

The Warrior Code of the Cavaliers

EDUCATION AND TRAINING

Even if there are enlightened leaders, if the people are not first educated and trained they cannot be employed.

Ancient education and training established a hierarchical order with distinct ranks, so that virtue and duty did not overstep each other, generalists and specialists did not obscure each other, daring and force did not encroach upon each other's domains. Thus power was united and minds were in harmony.

The Warrior Code of the Cavaliers

CIVIL AND MILITARY ORGANIZATION

In ancient times, the form of a nation was not incorporated into militias, and military forms were not incorporated into the state. Therefore virtue and duty did not overstep each other.

The Warrior Code of the Cavaliers

Unaffected People

Ancient leaders esteemed people who were not conceited; unaffected people were administrators of leadership. Since they were unaffected, they had no ambitions; and having no ambitions, they were not contentious. The true facts about conditions in a nation could be heard from them, and appropriate information about military affairs could be heard from them. Therefore generalists and specialists did not obscure each other.

The Warrior Code of the Cavaliers

Employment

Once you have educated and trained your people, then you may carefully select them for employment. When everything is as orderly as possible, all posts are filled. When education and training are as efficient as possible, the interests and initiatives of the people are wholesome. When customs are established, the body of the populace is normalized. This is what the influence of education can attain.

The Warrior Code of the Cavaliers

Security and Victory

The ancients did not pursue the fleeing far and did not chase down those in retreat. Because they did not go far, they were hard to lure; because they did not give chase, they were hard to entrap. They achieved security by courtesy and victory by humaneness. After they had won, their training could be re-used; that is why cultured people esteem it.

The Warrior Code of the Cavaliers

STERNNESS AND STRICTNESS

If the military is too stern, the people will be discouraged; if it is not strict enough, the people will not be victorious.

When the leadership works the people improperly, drafting peasants without regard to age and drafting artisans without regard to skills, and the officials in charge are contemptuous, this is called being too stern. Be too stern, and the people will be discouraged.

When the leadership does not honor the worthy but trusts deceivers and villains, does not honor the Way but trusts the bold and powerful, does not value those who follow orders but values those who disobey, does not value good conduct but values violence, and debases itself to officials, this is called insufficient strictness. If there is insufficient strictness, the people will not be victorious.

The Warrior Code of the Cavaliers

RELAXATION

Military operations should be relaxed in the main. When re-laxed, the strength of the people is full; even if they cross swords, the foot soldiers do not run, the chariots do not bolt; they do not break ranks to chase fleeing enemies and so do not lose order. The stability of a military operation is in not losing order, not using up the strength of man or beast, and not violating instructions in matters of pacing.

The Warrior Code of the Cavaliers

STATECRAFT AND MILITARY AFFAIRS

In ancient times, statecraft was not involved in military affairs, and militarism did not penetrate states. When militarism penetrates states, the virtues of the people wither away; when statecraft is involved in military affairs, the virtues of the people weaken.

Therefore in matters of state, discourse is cultured and speech is warm. At court, one is respectful and humble; one refines oneself and treats others accordingly. One does not go anywhere unless invited, does not speak unless asked; and one retires more readily than one steps forward.

In the military, one stands proudly and defiantly, versatile and effective in action. Warriors do not bow, war chariots do not go on parade in ceremonies. On the ramparts there are no manners; in emergencies there is no seniority.

Therefore, etiquette is to law as outside to inside; culture is to warriorhood as left is to right.

The Warrior Code of the Cavaliers

VIRTUES AND SKILLS

In ancient times, wise kings brought people's virtues to light and made full use of people's skills, so there were no neglected virtues and no negligent people. There was no reason to create rewards and no reason to apply penalties.

The Warrior Code of the Cavaliers

DETERIORATION OF CHARISMA

King Shun (r. 2255–2207 BCE) neither rewarded nor punished, yet his people were willingly useful; this is the epitome of charisma. The Xia dynasty (2205–1766 BCE) rewarded and did not punish; this is the epitome of education. The Yin dynasty (1766–1122 BCE) punished and did not reward; this is the epitome of authoritarianism. The Zhou dynasty (1122–256 BCE) relies on both reward and punishment; its charisma has deteriorated.

The Warrior Code of the Charioteers

IMMEDIATE FEEDBACK

Rewards are handed out immediately, so that the people may quickly gain the benefit of doing good. Punishments are executed on the spot, so that the people may quickly see the harm in doing wrong. The greatest good is not rewarded, so people do not become conceited about being good, either in the higher or lower echelons.

The Warrior Code of the Charioteers

HUMILITY

When the upper echelons are not conceited about being good, then they do not become haughty and overbearing;

when the lower echelons are not conceited about being good, then they are classless. When upper and lower echelons are thus not conceited about being good, this is the epitome of deference.

The Warrior Code of the Charioteers

FAILURE AND FAULT

Great failure is not punished, so that people in the upper and lower echelons attribute the fault to themselves. When the upper echelons attribute fault to themselves, they will repent of their errors; when the lower echelons attribute fault to themselves, they will avoid wrongdoing. When the upper and lower echelons share the negative in this way, that is the epitome of deference.

The Warrior Code of the Charioteers

HARMONY

In ancient times, fighting troops were not drafted for three years, seeing the toil of the people. Those in higher positions and those in lower positions were responsive to each other. Under these conditions, there was the epitome of harmony. When the aim was attained, they sang songs of triumph to show joy. Putting down arms and constructing spiritual monuments in response to the work of the people, they showed when to rest.

The Warrior Code of the Charioteers

Preparations

Whenever there is warfare, define ranks and positions, publish rewards and punishments, round up mercenaries, promulgate orders, inquire into public opinion, seek out the skilled, think analogically and find out about things, remove doubt and get rid of suspicion, nurture strength and look for skill, and go by the movement of hearts and minds.

When you are going to war, consolidate the masses, ascertain where advantage lies, govern the disorderly, cause the stalled to advance, get everyone to follow what is right and develop a sense of shame, streamline rules, and minimize punishments. Crack down on minor offenses, because if minor offenses prevail, major offenses will follow.

The Warrior Code of the Cavaliers

Five Considerations

Obey nature, amass goods, gladden the masses, take advantage of the lay of the land, and outfit the soldiers: these are called the five considerations.

To obey nature, act according to the season. To amass goods, plunder the enemy. To gladden the masses, be diligent. To take advantage of the lay of the land, guard narrow passes. To outfit the soldiers, provide bows and arrows for surrounding, spears and lances for defense, and pikes and halberds for standby.

Generally speaking, these five kinds of weapons have five appropriate uses. The longer-ranged are used to surround the shorter-ranged, the shorter-ranged are used to help out the longer-ranged. When they are used alternately in battle, then you can last a long time; when they are all used, then you are strong. When you use weaponry appropriate to what you see opponents using, this is called matching them.

The Warrior Code of the Cavaliers

STRATEGIC MEASUREMENTS

War is a national crisis; it is necessary to examine the grounds of death and life, and the ways to survival and extinction. Thus you measure militias in terms of five parameters, comparing them in terms of strategic measurements to find out the real situation. First is guidance. Second is climate. Third is ground. Fourth is leadership. Fifth is order.

Guidance is what induces popular accord with the rulership, so the people are willing to follow it to death and follow it in life, without opposition.

Climate refers to darkness and light, cold and heat, the structure of the seasons.

Grounds may be high or low, near or far, treacherous or easy, broad or narrow, deadly or viable.

Leadership is a matter of knowledge, trustworthiness, humaneness, valor, and strictness.

Order involves organizational structure, chain of command, and logistics.

All leaders have heard of these five things; those who know them prevail over those who do not. That is why we make comparisons in terms of strategic measurements, to find out the real situation. Which civil leadership has guidance? Which military leadership has ability? Whose climate and grounds are advantageous? Whose order is enforced?

Whose forces are stronger? Whose officers and soldiers are better trained? Whose rewards and punishments are clearer?

Sun Tzu's Art of War

SUBTERFUGE

One can assess advantages through listening, then take up an appropriate posture or make an appropriate disposition to bolster one's exterior.

To take up a posture or a disposition means to manipulate strategy according to advantage. Warfare is a path of subterfuge. That is why you make a show of incompetence when you are actually competent, make a show of ineffectiveness when you are in fact effective. When nearby you appear to be distant, and when distant you appear to be nearby.

Seducing opponents by prospects of gain, take them over by means of confusion. Even when you are solid, still be on the defensive; even when you are strong, be evasive. Use anger to make them upset, use humility to make them arrogant. Tire them while taking it easy, cause division among them while acting friendly. Attack where they are unprepared, emerge when they least expect it.

This means that the victories of warriors cannot be told of beforehand.

Sun Tzu's Art of War

CONTINGENCY PLANNING

Those who figure out how to win before doing battle have the majority of advantageous plans, while those whose schemes prove to be failures even before battle have the fewer advantageous plans. Those with many such plans win, those with few such plans lose; there is no need to even mention those with no such plans. When I view a situation in this way, it becomes evident who will win and who will lose.

Sun Tzu's Art of War

EFFICIENCY

In actual combat, what is important is to win; go on too long, and you blunt your troops and snap your edge. Besiege a citadel, and your strength is depleted; keep an army in the field too long, and the resources of the nation will be insufficient. When you blunt your troops, snap your edge, deplete your strength, and exhaust resources, then rivals will arise to take advantage of your predicament. Then it will be impossible to effect a good ending, even with knowledge.

Therefore in military affairs we may hear of being clumsy but swift, while we never see the skillful prolonging an action. This is because a nation never benefits from prolonging a military action.

Sun Tzu's Art of War

BALANCE

Those who are not completely aware of drawbacks of military action cannot be completely aware of advantages in military action.

Sun Tzu's Art of War

Economic Consequences of Warfare

The reason that nations are impoverished by their armies is that those who send their armies far away ship goods far away, and when goods are shipped far away, the farmers grow poor. Those who are near the army sell dear, and because of high prices money runs out. When the money runs out, there is increased pressure to appropriate things for military use, exhausting the heartland, draining the households.

Sun Tzu's Art of War

Keeping Intact

The general rule for military operations is that keeping a nation intact is best, while destroying a nation is next; keeping a militia intact is best, destroying a militia is next. Keeping a battalion intact is best, destroying a battalion is next. Keeping a company intact is best, destroying a company is next. Keeping a squad intact is best, destroying a squad is next.

Sun Tzu's Art of War

Foiling Opponents

One hundred percent victory in battle is not the finest skill; foiling others' military operations without even fighting is the finest skill.

Sun Tzu's Art of War

Four Levels of Attack

A superior military operation attacks planning, the next best attacks alliances; the next attacks armed forces, the lowest attacks cities.

Sun Tzu's Art of War

Planning Attack

When a military leader cannot contain anger and has his men swarm the citadel, this kills a third of his soldiers; and with the citadel still not taken, this is a fiasco of a siege. Therefore, one who uses the military skillfully foils the military operations of others without fighting, takes others' citadels without attacking, and crushes others' states without taking a long time, making sure to remain intact to contend with the world, so that his forces are not blunted and the advantage can be complete. This is the rule for planning attack.

Sun Tzu's Art of War

Firmness and Stubbornness

Thus what would be firmness in the face of a small opponent will get you captured by a large opponent.

Sun Tzu's Art of War

Knowing Winners

There are five ways to know winners. Those who know when to fight and when not to fight are winners. Those who know the uses of large and small groups are winners. Those whose upper and lower echelons have the same desires are winners. Those who await the unprepared with preparedness are winners. Those whose military leaders are capable and not dominated by the civilian leaders are winners. These five items are ways to know winners.

So it is said that if you know others and know yourself, you will not be imperiled in a hundred battles. If you do not know others but do know yourself, you will win some and lose some. If you do not know others and do not know yourself, you will be imperiled in every battle.

Sun Tzu's Art of War

INVINCIBILITY AND VULNERABILITY

The ancients who were skilled in combat first became invincible, and in that condition awaited vulnerability on the part of enemies. Invincibility is up to you yourself; vulnerability depends on the opponent. Therefore those who are skilled in combat can become invincible but cannot make opponents vulnerable to certain defeat. This is why it is said that victory can be discerned but cannot be made.

Invincibility is a matter of defense, vulnerability is a matter of offense. When you defend, it is because you are outgunned; when you attack, it is because the opponent is no match.

Those skilled at defense hide in the deepest depths of the earth; those skilled at offense maneuver in the highest heights of the sky. Thus they can preserve themselves and make victory complete.

Sun Tzu's Art of War

INCONSPICUOUS SUCCESS

Those considered good warriors in ancient times were those who won when it was easy to win. Thus the victories of good warriors have nothing extraordinary about them: they are not famed for brilliance, not accorded merit for bravado. Thus their victories in battle are not in doubt. They are not in doubt because the measures they take are sure to win, since they are overcoming those who have already lost.

Sun Tzu's Art of War

VICTORY AND DEFEAT

Therefore those who are skilled in combat take a stand on an invincible ground without losing sight of opponents' vulnerabilities. Thus a victorious militia wins before ever seeking to do battle, while a defeated militia seeks victory after it has already gotten into a fight.

When those who employ military forces will put the Way into practice and keep its laws, they can thereby judge the outcome. The laws are as follows: first is measure, second is capacity, third is order, fourth is efficacy, fifth is victory. The ground gives rise to measures, measures produce capacity. Capacity gives rise to order, order produces efficacy. Efficacy gives rise to victory.

Thus a victorious militia is like a weight balanced against another weight that is five hundred times less, while a defeated militia is like a weight balanced against another weight that is five hundred times more. Those who get the people to fight from a winning position are as though opening up dammed waters into a mile-deep canyon; this is a matter of the formation of force.

Sun Tzu's Art of War

ORGANIZATION AND OPERATION

What normally makes managing a large group similar to managing a small group is a system of order. What makes fighting a large group similar to fighting a small group is the use of emblems and signals. What enables military forces to take on enemies without defeat is the implementation of surprise tactics as well as conventional strategies. What makes a military intervention as effective as a stone thrown onto eggs is discernment of openings and solidity.

Sun Tzu's Art of War

SURPRISE TACTICS

Usually battle is engaged in a conventional manner but is won by surprise tactics. So those who are good at surprise maneuvers are endless as sky and earth, inexhaustible as the great rivers, finishing, then starting again, as epitomized by the sun and moon, dying and then being born again, as epitomized by the four seasons.

Sun Tzu's Art of War

MOMENTUM

The fact that the velocity of rushing water can reach the point where it can sweep away boulders is due to momentum; the fact that the strike of a bird of prey can attain a crushing force is due to timing and control. Thus those skilled at combat make sure their momentum is closely channeled and their timing closely controlled. Their momentum is like drawing a catapult, their timing and control are like pulling the trigger. In the midst of confusion they fight wildly without being thrown into disarray; in the midst of chaos their formations are versatile, so they cannot be defeated.

Sun Tzu's Art of War

PARADOX AND LOGIC

Rebellion arises from orderliness, cowardice arises from bravado, weakness arises from strength. Whether there is order or unruliness depends on the operative logic of the order. Bravery and cowardice depend on the configurations and momentum of power. Strength and weakness depend on formation.

Sun Tzu's Art of War

MANEUVERING OTHERS

Those who are good at maneuvering enemies mold them into specific formations, to which the enemies may be sure to conform. Give opponents an opportunity they are sure to take, maneuvering them in this way, then wait in ambush for them.

Sun Tzu's Art of War

DISPOSITION OF FORCE

For these reasons, those who are skilled in combat look to disposition of force and momentum; they do not put the onus on individual people. That is why they can choose people yet put their trust in momentum.

To rely on momentum is to get people to go into battle like rolling logs and rocks. By nature, logs and rocks remain still on even ground and roll when the ground is steep; they remain stationary when square, they roll when round.

The momentum of people who are good at combat is like rolling round rocks down a high mountain, because of the disposition of force.

Sun Tzu's Art of War

Taking a Stand

Generally speaking, those who have taken up their position on a battlefield first and await the enemy there are fresh, while those who take up their position on a battlefield last and thus rush into combat are wearied. Therefore skilled warriors bring others to them and do not go to others.

Sun Tzu's Art of War

Seducing Enemies

What effectively induces enemies to come of their own accord is the prospect of gain; what effectively prevents enemies from coming is the threat of harm. So to effectively tire a rested enemy, starve a well-fed one, or stir up a calm one is a matter of going where the enemy is sure to give chase.

Sun Tzu's Art of War

Successful Attack and Defense

Those who always take what they besiege do so by attacking where there is no defense. Those whose defense always stands firm defend where attack is certain.

Therefore a good attack is one against which an enemy does not know where to defend, while a good defense is one against which an enemy does not know where to attack. Be subtle, subtle even to the point of formlessness; be mysterious, mysterious even to the point of soundlessness: thus you can control the enemy's fate.

Sun Tzu's Art of War

Advance and Retreat

To advance unstoppably, strike at openings. To retreat elusively, move too fast to be caught up with. Thus, when you want to fight, the way to make an enemy have no choice but to fight with you, even though he is secure behind high ramparts and deep moats, is to attack where the enemy is sure to go to the rescue. When you don't want to fight, to make an enemy unable to fight with you even if you are only defending a line drawn in the ground, divert his aim.

Sun Tzu's Art of War

Concentration and Division

If you induce others to adopt a form while you remain formless, then you will be concentrated while the enemy will be divided. When you are concentrated and thus united, whereas the enemy is divided into ten, that means you are attacking with ten times his strength, so you are a large contingent while the enemy is in small groups. If you can attack small groups with a larger contingent, then you will have fewer to fight against at a time.

Sun Tzu's Art of War

DISABLING DEFENSES

Your battleground should be unknown, because if it is unknown, then the enemy will have to post many defensive positions, and when the enemy has to man many defensive positions, then you will have fewer people to fight against at a time.

Thus when they are manned in front, they are undermanned in the rear; when they are manned in the rear, they are undermanned in front. When manned at the left, they are undermanned to the right; when manned at the right, they are undermanned to the left.

When they are manned everywhere, they are undermanned everywhere. Those who are undermanned are those who are on the defensive against others; those who have plenty of personnel are those who cause others to be on the defensive against them.

Sun Tzu's Art of War

EXAMINING ENEMIES

When you plot against others to discern winning and losing strategies, you work on them to discern their patterns of action. You induce them to adopt specific formations to discern deadly and viable grounds, you skirmish with them to discern where they are sufficient and where they are lacking.

Sun Tzu's Art of War

FORM

When you plan victory for the masses based on formation, the masses cannot discern it; everyone knows the form of your victory, but no one knows the form by which you achieved victory. This is why a victory in battle is not repeated; adaptive formation is of endless scope.

The formation of a militia is symbolized by water. Water travels away from higher places toward lower places; military victory is a matter of avoiding the solid and striking at openings. The course of water is determined by earth; the way to military victory depends on the opponent.

Thus a militia has no permanently fixed configuration, no constant form. Those who are able to seize victory by adapting to opponents are called experts.

No element is always dominant, no season is always present. Some days are shorter, some are longer; the moon wanes away and then reappears.

Sun Tzu's Art of War

FORMLESSNESS

The consummate formation of a militia is to reach formlessness. Where there is no specific form, even deeply placed agents cannot spy it out; even the canny strategist cannot scheme against it.

Sun Tzu's Art of War

INTELLIGENCE NEEDS

Those who do not know the plans of competitors cannot enter capably into preliminary negotiations; those who do not know the lay of the land cannot maneuver a militia; those who do not use local guides cannot gain the advantages of the terrain.

Sun Tzu's Art of War

SPIRIT AND HEART

The armed forces may have their spirits taken away, while the generals may have their heart taken away.

In this connection, in the morning spirits are keen, in the afternoon spirits fade, in the evening spirits wane away.

Good warriors avoid keen spirits, instead striking enemies when their spirits are fading and waning. This is the mastery of mood.

To face confusion with composure and face clamor with calm is the mastery of heart.

Sun Tzu's Art of War

STRENGTH AND ADAPTATION

To stay close to home to face those who come from far away, to face the weary in a condition of ease, to face the hungry with full stomachs, is the mastery of strength. Not to stand in the way of an orderly march, and not to attack an impeccable battle line, is the mastery of adaptation.

Sun Tzu's Art of War

RULES FOR MILITARY OPERATIONS

Rules for military operations:

Don't face high ground.
Don't get backed up against a hill.
Don't pursue a feigned retreat.
Don't attack fresh troops.
Don't chase after decoys.
Don't try to stop an army on the way home.
Leave a way out for a surrounded army.
Don't press a desperate enemy.

Sun Tzu's Art of War